NO FEAR RETIREMENT

HOW TO ENJOY A FUN-FILLED AND FULFILLING LIFE WHEN YOU RETIRE

PAMELA HOUGHTON

RƎTHINK PRESS

First published in Great Britain 2015
by Rethink Press (www.rethinkpress.com)

Praise

'Written with a wealth of personal experience and knowledge, *No Fear Retirement* is an excellent resource. Whether you are a rejoicing retiree or a reluctant retiree, expect to find great value in reading this book. Taking time to reflect on the Pause for Thought questions along the twelve phases of retirement will make the book even more worthwhile.'

Paul G. Ward

President, 2Young2Retire, LLC. www.2Young2Retire.com

'Pamela Houghton has written a stellar book on retirement; not only is it practically informative but, much more to the point, it moves you to reflect deeply on what is your 'heart's desire'. With obvious wisdom and aplomb she guides you to step back from your life a bit and seriously consider just how you plan to construct a new life structure that serves you best during your 'illumination years'. Our current cultural definition of retirement many times fails to enliven the heart and bring joy to our spirit; actually it can do the opposite. Pamela Houghton gives you a new definition of retirement that frees you to live fully and meaningfully. She challenges you to consider what factors of personality and character support a new retirement experience that offers deep meaning and purpose, and can foster the profound consolation of 'significance beyond success'. I recommend her book for all those who long to live life from the center of their being.'

Dr. Richard P Johnson

Founder of Retirement Options www.retirementoptions.com

Contents

Introduction
Who Should Read This Book?

Anyone who is seeking a fun-filled and fear-free retirement

If you already have your retirement mapped out, and you know exactly what you are going to do with your time, this book will help you to check that all your plans are in place and all your boxes are ticked.

If you are nervous about retiring, or just not sure how you want to spend your retirement years, then this book will ensure that you focus on your future and remove any obstacles in the way of a happy and successful retirement.

If you are already retired, but retirement is proving a disappointment, then this book will provide you with some ideas for a change of direction.

Why Did I Write This Book?

One summer my university decided it could no longer afford to employ the number of academics it was paying, and my career and working life came to an abrupt end after nearly fifty years. I had enjoyed every day of my working life, although not necessarily every part of every day! It had been challenging but hugely enjoyable. I had been surrounded by interesting and interested colleagues. There was a structure to my day (and sometimes evenings and weekends). There was an effortless convenience in maintaining the continuity and comfort of my friendships at work on a daily basis. I was part of a great team with a shared sense of making a difference to the lives of our students.

Although I knew I would have to retire one day I was not ready at that particular time and I panicked. I was afraid of retirement. I was lucky enough to have my finances in place, but I looked around for some sort of support to see me through what I regarded as a painful transition into this new and significant phase of my life. What was I going to do with my time? Where was I going to do it? How would I resist falling into things I would not enjoy?

The more I understood the emotional and psychological consequences of retirement the more I realised that I was not alone with my fears. I discovered that there are many people, like me, who have fears about retirement. Each chapter of this book addresses one of these top ten fears that have been most frequently expressed:

R   replacement – How can I replace the benefits I get from working?

E   expectations – What can I expect during my transition from work to retirement?

T   time – How will I spend my time?

I   identity – Who will I become once I am retired?

R   relationships – How will my relationships change?

E   enjoyment and happiness – How can I find enjoyment and happiness in what I have?

M   meaning and purpose – Will I find meaning and purpose in my retirement?

E   enough – Will I have enough money to do what I want to do?*

N   new location – Should I move somewhere new?

T   taking care – How should I take care of myself?

*This book does not claim to give you financial advice. What this chapter gives you is an opportunity to reflect on the things you want to do in your retirement, what it will cost to do them, and whether you will have 'enough' money to do what you want.

Summary

Retirement provides us with unlimited possibilities and each of our experiences will be unique. It provides us with a final opportunity to re-kindle old passions, discover who we really are, and balance an appreciation of our personal strengths and talents with the needs of the world around us. If we are not to waste this time then we should face our fears and re-frame those aspects of our life that could obstruct what we want to achieve in our third age.

This book has been written for anyone who wants to be forewarned about the consequences of giving up work so that they can make an informed choice about when to retire, and how to put plans in place to enjoy a happy and successful retirement. It has been predominantly written for those who are:

- ☼ Considering the option of taking full or partial retirement
- ☼ Already actively and happily planning for retirement
- ☼ Reluctant retirees harbouring fears about retirement
- ☼ New, and possibly disappointed retirees

Although it has been written for both men and women, there is a particular aspect of retirement that can affect women more than men. This is the caring role. There is a danger that the 'baby boomer' generation of women, who have worked for half a century managing a career, home and family, will find it difficult to resist the expectations of family and government to take on the multiple roles of elder care, spouse care, adult child care, and grandchild care when they retire.

This book will emphasise the need for such temptations to be balanced with a sense of entitlement to pursue their own personal passions and dreams also.

Why Should You Read This Book?

My aim is that when you have finished reading this book you will have:

- ○ Reviewed your own personal expectations for a successful retirement
- ○ Sought guidance from those who have successfully retired before you
- ○ Devised strategies to manage the expectations others have of you
- ○ Systematically focussed on facing your retirement concerns and fears
- ○ Revived personal passions and dreams
- ○ Prioritised meaning and purpose
- ○ Found entitlement to fun and enjoyment in retirement

Chapter 1 focuses on the first fear: *'How will I Replace the benefits I get from working?'* In addition to the financial rewards there are other less obvious benefits that we may take for granted while working, and may not even be aware of until they are no longer there. Each is so significant that they will be covered in more detail in other chapters.

- ○ Work gives us a structure to our life, helps us to manage our *Time*, and keeps us connected with the outside world.

○ At work we are normally rewarded for the skills and experience we bring, and the role we perform brings with it a personal sense of *Identity* and status.

○ Work provides us with constant contact with our colleagues with very little effort on our part. These *Relationships* can sometimes turn into deep and long lasting friendships, which inevitably change when we retire.

○ Work also provides us with some *Meaning* and purpose to our lives and a sense of satisfaction at the end of the day.

The fears associated with Time, Identity, Relationships, Meaning and Money will be covered in chapters three, four, five, seven and eight.

Chapter 2 focuses on the second fear: '*What can I expect during my transition from work to retirement?*' Our attitude towards ageing and retirement will determine the extent to which we will feel in control of the changes ahead of us and will feel satisfied with this next life phase. Changes that retirement bring to our closest relationships with family and dependents will also be covered in Chapter 5: 'How will my Relationships change?' While you have been busy planning your retirement in your mind, it is inevitable that those close to you will also have been planning your time and their expectations of you. This will be a time for transparency, honest conversations and an expectations exchange, to ensure that your own plans are not hijacked by others.

Chapter 6 asks: '*How can I find Enjoyment and Happiness in what I have?*' and examines the difference between pleasure, enjoyment and happiness, and the pursuit of personal happiness during retirement.

Chapter 9 focuses on: '*Should I move somewhere New?*' and explores the implications of moving house, moving out of the area, moving nearer children, and changing living conditions.

Chapter 10 considers the final fear: '*How should I Take care of myself?*' and focuses on health and well-being issues. This is an aspect of our life over which we feel we have little control, but the chapter will examine the role that health perception plays, and the precautions that can be taken to improve our overall wellbeing by making a daily plan.

1

REPLACEMENT

Celebrating Retirement and Replacing the Benefits of Working

FACTS

UK population:

- ○ For the first time in history there are now more people in the UK aged sixty and above than there are under eighteen
- ○ There are more pensioners than there are children under sixteen
- ○ There are 11 million people aged sixty-five and over (1/6th of the population)

Projected population:

- ○ By 2034 the number of over sixty-fives will rise to 16 million (23.5% of the population)
- ○ By 2086 one third of UK population will be over sixty
- ○ Nearly one in five people currently in the UK will live to see their 100th birthday

Source: Later Life in the United Kingdom – Age UK – May 2015

The Spanish translation of 'retirement' is '*jubilacion*' which is so much more uplifting and fits into the modern concept of retirement as something to be celebrated. This is a particularly exciting time to be considering retirement because the *definition, shape* and the *expectations* we have of retirement are changing significantly. The reason for this is that we are wealthier than previous generations as the increase in national wealth is being realised through our individual pensions, personal savings and the capital we have gained from the substantial increase in the value of our homes during our life time. We are healthier at retirement than previous generations as our normal life expectancy is now extended for several years without the handicap of physical limitations. For most of us retirement is the time when we no longer have responsibility for childcare or the need for paid employment, and without those obligations our time is now our own. Our age group at retirement is wealthier and healthier than ever before and we are able to shape our lives to suit ourselves.

Retirement can therefore provide us with our final opportunity to do new things, do things differently, or continue to do more of the things we enjoy. It can give us the chance to re-kindle old passions, explore wider horizons, meet new challenges, and find out who we really are. It can give us more time to use our existing talents and the experience we gained from working, to meet the needs of the world around us. Or it can provide us with the opportunity to continue to live the way we have always lived, but at a more leisurely pace, and with more time to do the things we have always enjoyed.

First, the *definition* of retirement is changing. The idea of completely withdrawing from work, retiring, at a specific age came into existence in the UK in 1908 when the first pension was paid. It was paid to those aged seventy or more with an annual income of £21 per year or less. However, at that time average life expectancy was around age fifty, only one in four people reached the age of seventy, and so many people would not live to claim their five shillings (25p) a week. Nevertheless it was a big improvement on what had happened in the past, when most people had to work until they died, rely on the paternalism of their employers, fall back on the Parish Poor Relief, or be supported by their family.

Since then, that withdrawal from work suddenly at a specific age, until recently defined as sixty-five for men and sixty for women, has contributed not only to society's view of retirement, but also the ageing process, and its expectations of what older workers and retirees can and cannot do.

The Government's changes to the State Pension Age has affected expectations and behaviour with many fifty to seventy-five year-olds now easing into retirement as a phased or gradual 'pre-tirement' process as outlined in Zopa and Consumer Intelligence Report rather than stopping work on a pre-specified date.

Retirement is no longer defined simply as a single event or point in time tied to a specific age, but as a process consisting of a number of phases. Age discrimination legislation prescribes that there is no longer even a specific age for retirement. For many, the years leading up to and beyond a normal retirement age, are now becoming a phased or gradual process.

This is happening for a number of reasons including a wish to retire earlier; a recognition that longer retirement requires more income; acknowledgement of current low return on savings; a desire and ability to remain physically and mentally active into later years and enhanced leisure opportunity expectations. Working beyond normal retirement age, changing career, reducing working hours or taking up new challenges or opportunities have become the norm for many. The retirement process for each of us is individual, and each phase within the process is unique, open to our own personal interpretation of planning, and our own search for meaning, purpose and satisfaction.

This shift has not only changed how society has seen retirement and the over sixty-fives it has also impacted on how we see ourselves in retirement. The old idea of retirement as a time only for rest and relaxation, with little need for any future planning or clarification of purpose is fast disappearing.

Second, retirement is changing its *shape*. We are retiring earlier, we are living longer, and because the Baby Boomers' generation (born between 1946 and 1964) has been reaching sixty-five, the percentage of over sixty-five year-olds is increasing. There are more sixty-five year-olds in the UK now than at any point in history. The first detailed analysis of returns from the 2011 census show that the overall number of people turning sixty-five that year leapt by 30% in a single year in the UK. Although the numbers retiring will then reduce slightly, there will still be well over 600,000 people turning sixty-five each year until at least 2018 and overall 3.3 million people are poised to hit state pension age in the next five years.

Because we are retiring earlier but we are living longer, retirement no longer consists of either full-time work or no-work. Retirees are choosing to dip in and out of the workplace, sometimes part-time, sometimes voluntary, and sometimes self-employed. Others have to do so from financial necessity.

Third, there is a change in the *expectations* that we ourselves have of retirement. The old perceptions and stereotyping of retirement as an end in itself have been replaced by a much more optimistic, energetic and unlimited view of the potential of both the older worker and of retirement. We can look to retirement for freedom. It provides us with the opportunity and freedom to choose what we want to do rather than have it prescribed for us by society. In this brave new world of retirement there is no need for us to be constrained by traditional stereotypes.

The most extensive surveys on attitudes to retirement have been undertaken by European Union institutions (European Commission in 2012). The results show that over half of respondents do not want to work beyond state pension age, but sixty-five per cent want to retire gradually. The average expected retirement age, based on current employment in the UK is 62.8, but this result hides a high proportion of people, 31%, expecting to work into their late sixties and even a significant proportion, 11%, expecting to work beyond seventy. At 64.9, self-employed people had an expected retirement age significantly above the average.

Earlier we painted an optimistic picture of the freedom and choice we have in retirement with its potential for being one of the most enjoyable stages of our life. However, not everyone feels so optimistic about it and some harbour concerns and fears about what they will do when they finally give up work. These doubts are understandable as there are a number of benefits that work provides for us:

- Work provides the financial means to build a home, bring up a family, support our leisure and interests, and make provision for our retirement.
- Work gives a structure to our life, helps us to manage our time, and keeps us connected with the outside world.
- Work can reward us for our skills and experience. What we earn also puts a value on it, and the role we perform brings with it a personal sense of identity and status.
- Work can provide companionship and constant contact with other people on a daily basis without much effort required on our part. These relationships can sometimes turn into deep and long lasting friendships that inevitably change when we are no longer working with them each day.
- Work can provide us with a sense of satisfaction at the end of the day and a meaning and purpose to our lives.

....

PAUSE FOR THOUGHT
Consider each of these benefits in turn
- *Which benefits from work are you likely/do you to miss the most?*
- *How could you replace the financial rewards, structure, career identity, companionship, and sense of satisfaction in preparation for/in retirement?*

....

It is therefore unrealistic to think that we can move out of work one day and move into our new life of retirement the next day without our own 'snagging' list of things in our lives, to which we need to pay attention.

Below are some examples of the recurring statements that can be heard from the newly retired:

- ○ 'When I was working I had constant contact with my colleagues and thought of some of them as friends. Since I left work my colleagues have stopped emailing and phoning me and I feel our friendships no longer have the same value.'
- ○ 'When I was at work I knew exactly what I had to do each day and there was a beginning, middle and end to my week. Now I am being pulled in all directions and end up doing none of the things I want to do.'

- ○ 'I feel I am just filling up my days and keeping busy to avoid getting bored.'
- ○ 'When I was at work I had a sense of who I was and I had a certain status. I feel uncomfortable in the role of just a retiree and I don't know how to make myself sound interesting when I meet someone new.'
- ○ 'My partner, my family and I are now falling out and falling over ourselves all the time.'
- ○ 'Retirement is costing more than I expected.'
- ○ 'When I was working I felt a sense of achievement at the end of most days from a day well spent. Now that I am no longer working I feel there is little meaning and purpose to my life and I don't get that same sense of achievement.'
- ○ 'I am just not enjoying my retirement in the way that I thought I would. It is not making me happy.'
- ○ 'We have moved to our idyllic retirement location but it is not turning out as successfully as we expected.'
- ○ 'I have often felt quite low since I retired.'

....

PAUSE FOR THOUGHT

- – *Have you heard such comments from the people you know who are retired?*
- – *Have they resolved their issues? If so, how?*

....

The purpose of this book is to:

- ○ Provide the time and space for us to make sense of what is happening
- ○ Take the opportunity to discover what we really want from our retirement
- ○ Forewarn us of the steps we can take to avoid, or minimise, any unnecessary obstacles as we are moving through the transition from work to retirement

Whether you are still considering retirement, or have already retired, this book will help you to shape the retirement you want. Because there is so much choice in retirement we can make the most of it by being proactive and thinking ahead rather than allowing retirement to happen to us. It will give us the opportunity to visualise how it will look and feel; how we want to spend our time; who we want to share our time with; how much money we will need to do the things we want; who we want to be now that we are grown up; where we want to live; and how we can stay well enough to do the things we want.

So this book is not only about retirement but also about us. Retirement should not be regarded in isolation as something we do, but a happy retiree should also consider who they are. It gives us the opportunity to consider in an open and honest way where our expectations and concerns may lay. It also gives us the opportunity to exchange expectations with those around us so that we hear and understand the views of those who will be sharing our retirement.

When going through this process of self-reflection it is often helpful to share and discuss our thoughts with others who may have been through the same transition from work to retirement. The Pauses for Thought help you to do this. These may be people we have known, and have known us for years, so that discussing with them, and others we value, will help us to pass more smoothly through this process.

If we can deal with our concerns and stop them taking over then we will feel more optimistic about the future. If we leave our concerns unexamined then we are unlikely to make changes and take control of our own future.

....

PAUSE FOR THOUGHT

Divide this circle up into segments and write in each
segment one expectation you have of your retirement.
Indicate its level of importance by marking each segment
with a line (the further away from the centre the more
important it is to you)

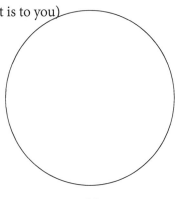

....

PAUSE FOR THOUGHT

Write in each segment one of the ten fears. Once again make a small line to indicate your current level of satisfaction with each area (the further away from the centre the more satisfied you are)

1. My ability to replace my work benefits
2. The expectations I have of my retirement (see previous prompt)
3. How I will spend my time
4. My ability to replace my career identity with a new identity
5. My relationships
6. My daily level of enjoyment and happiness
7. Meaning and purpose in my life
8. My finances
9. Where I now live
10. My level of physical, mental, social and spiritual well-being

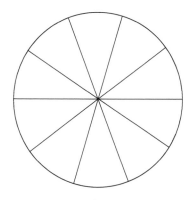

....

PAUSE FOR THOUGHT

– *What do you think are the necessary components of a*
  successful retirement for you?
– *What are the life positives you see in your own retirement?*
– *What are the life challenges you see in your own*
  retirement?

....

The next chapter will take us through the various phases we can
expect to experience during the transition from work to retirement.

2

EXPECTATIONS

What Can I Expect
During My Transition
From Work to Retirement?

Aspirations for later life

Looking particularly at those aged fifty to fifty-nine – that is, those in the decade leading up to when they are sixty or more – only around half (53%) said they had hopes or ambitions. This, therefore, shows that a significant proportion (47%) of this group had either not thought about it that much or not thought about it at all.

Source: Later Life in the United Kingdom – Age UK – May 2015

PAUSE FOR THOUGHT

– *What phase of retirement transition are you in right now? Circle the phase below.*

1 2 3 4 5 6 7 8 9 10 11 12

(adapted from Richard P. Johnson, PhD – *The New Retirement*)

1. Normal Career – retirement not genuinely considered
2. Remote phase – retirement considered as a possibility
3. Near phase – retirement considered as a probability

Pre-Retirement

4. First doubts phase
5. Decision making phase

6. Visualising the Future phase
7. Acknowledgement and Acceptance phase
8. Disengagement/Exit

Post retirement
9. Honeymoon phase– post retirement, all is bliss!
10. Rest and Relaxation phase– settling into a quieter time
11. Disenchantment phase – find lots wrong with retirement and may want to reverse your decision
12. Reorientation and Routine in retirement – develop attitude of satisfaction and contentment in retirement

As human beings we encounter transitions throughout our life as we live through the life phases of infancy into childhood, into adolescence, into adulthood, and into middle age. Transitions exist within each of the life phases and the movement from one to another can provide us with substantial demands and challenges, but also new opportunities. Each of us handles these transitions in our own unique way by developing coping strategies to help us manage and overcome the obstacles we encounter.

William Bridges in *Transitions: Making Sense of Life's Changes* described three phases of transition: the endings, the neutral zone and the new beginnings. During the first phase we should decide what is ending and what is continuing through the transition. This is similar to how we feel when we go through the process of mourning in which in order to manage transition we have to accept the reality of losses. Once we have decided what is ending we are able to see what we can give up, what we should replace, what we can define differently, and what we want to carry from our past into our new future. During the second phase of transition, the neutral zone, we are still uncertain about the future and this phase will take some time whilst we reflect on the past and adjust to our redefined future. The third phase in transition is the time for new beginnings and where we learn to adjust to a new chapter in our life. Transition takes time and everyone moves through the phases at different speeds.

PAUSE FOR THOUGHT
- *When did you last have to adjust to a transition?*
- *How did you overcome any obstacles?*
- *What experience can you carry forward with you to ease your transition into retirement?*

PAUSE FOR THOUGHT
- *Who do you know that has made a successful transition from work to retirement?*
- *Are you able to seek their views and get some tips from them?*

We spend most of our early life working through education towards a career, then many years acquiring the relevant experience and skills, finally establishing a career identity. Over the years, the significant contributions we will have made to the well-being of our family and friends, our workplace and more generally to society, will have given us a sense of achievement.

Retirement is both a transitional event and a life stage phase. When it comes it is a transition into a whole new phase of our life.

For some, retirement is the time of our life for which we have planned, and to which we have looked forward with eager anticipation for many years. For others, particularly those who have enjoyed their work, and would have chosen to continue if they could, the transition into retirement can be a very stressful experience. Others feel neutral about retirement, have no particular plans and just expect opportunities to turn up and come to them.

If we are someone who has always had many other things going on in our life, in addition to work, before retirement, then we may settle into retirement quickly and easily. However, if we have allowed work to be our major focus then it is sensible to undertake some pre-retirement planning so that when we finally disengage from work we can minimise any distress we may feel during our transition from work into retirement. Before we retire we can go through a number of phases.

PAUSE FOR THOUGHT
- *If you are about to retire can you recognise the phase you are currently going through as you read through the next section?*
- *What advice would you give to others in the future who maybe going through the same experience during transition?*

Preparing for Retirement – Pre-Retirement
- First doubts phase
- Decision making phase
- Visualising the future phase
- Acknowledgement and Acceptance phase
- Exit from work phase

First doubts phase
Our retirement date maybe clearly earmarked, agreed well in advance, and no likelihood of either party changing their mind. If, however, the choice of timing is left to us, the *first doubts phase* can start the process. The possibility of retirement occurs when we start to feel vaguely discontent with our work but may have not yet clarified the cause. These doubts, some are listed here although there are undoubtedly others, can be triggered by any number of events:
- Incidental and unplanned changes within the organisation we work in, which can cause uncertainty

- Planned changes by the organisation intended to create uncertainty
- Feeling of professional burnout
- Sudden lack of confidence in our ability
- Changes in work relationships prompted by a new boss or new team member
- A specific event that causes the feeling of discontent
- Partner's or friend's retirement
- Partner's or friend's premature incapacity or death
- Incident in leisure life stimulates our own lack of interest in work

These doubts lead to behaviour which is initially unconscious but can indicate to others our gradual discontent with work. As we become more confident about our doubts we will ignore negative reactions from others and seek out individuals who will reinforce those doubts. Getting a negative reaction can slow down our process of decision making about whether to retire but positive reinforcement about our doubts can hasten it.

Some careers involve more than one role and by relinquishing our career role it has a knock on effect for a variety of different roles and other aspects of our lives. For a clergyman or members of the Armed Services, for example, giving up work may also mean giving up a home, the area in which the family lives, certain standing in society, positions on a number of local committees and membership of a tightly defined group of very like-minded colleagues. In these situations it is particularly important to understand the implications of having to exit a number of roles simultaneously, as the decision to retire may have to be total and not reversable.

Decision making phase

The *decision making phase* is the opportunity to pursue all the various options and alternatives open to us and weigh up the pros and cons of retirement or partial retirement. As these are significant decisions, so during this phase it is important to look for support and the widest possible guidance. As the options begin to narrow we start to change the reference group we use to discuss our retirement options and seek the view of others. Any positive support we receive for our decision from those around us acts as a reality test and provides assurance that our concerns about our work, and doubting our commitment to it, are justified. Other people may suggest alternatives to our work options that we can start seriously considering as possible retirement opportunities.

Visualising the future phase

In the *visualising the future phase*, we visualise ourselves taking up these alternative options for a happy and successful retirement. We see ourself taking on a new identity and become aware that our old role and identity is no longer appropriate or satisfactory. We have the opportunity to do and be something different. Those retirees who have had the opportunity to weigh alternatives and go through a conscious process of decision making tend to experience greater enjoyment after leaving work and adjust to their new identity more easily.

Obviously, those first doubts and the decision making process will be played out differently if our retirement is not from our own choice and the adjustment can be more difficult. The exit and disengagement from work in this situation will be made easier for us if we are not being singled out within our workplace, but are experiencing the retirement process as part of a group. There is great benefit to be had from being part of a group and it is worth putting effort into maintaining contact, using it for ongoing support during the transition. If we are being singled out and feel isolated and alone in our decision, this is a good time to seek professional guidance.

Acknowledgement and Acceptance phase

If we have not started to build bridges between our working world and our retirement world before we retire then the *acknowledgement and acceptance phase* can feel both exciting and very disorientating. We have one foot in our past and one in our future. However, the process of establishing a new identity is made easier and occurs more quickly if we have already started to acknowledge and accept the reality of the situation, visualise our new identity and practise the integration of our past into our new identity. The sooner we go public and start exhibiting the characteristics of our new identity the sooner those around us will start to see us differently.

Disengagement/Exit from work phase

The *exit from work phase* involves a shift from all the aspects of our working life that we may have taken for granted for a very long time. These include freedom to make choices about how we use our time; changes to our career identity; learning to deal with the reactions of others to our new status in retirement; adjusting to a different type of relationship with our work colleagues; seeking out new reference groups; and creating new friendship groups.

In many cases we will be handing over our job to someone else but at the same time having no handover ourselves to help us with our transition into retirement.

As we move from work into retirement we should accept the need to spend time making sense of what is happening and to take the opportunity to discover what we really want from our retirement.

Everyone's experience of retirement is different but some retirees have reported that they can go through some, or all, of the following phases when they first retire and before they settle down to the retirement routine of choice. These phases are not necessarily sequential.

....

PAUSE FOR THOUGHT

- *If you are already retired can you recognise the phase you are currently going through as you read through the next section?*
- *What advice would you give to others in the future who may be going through the same experience?*

....

Retirement

- ○ The Honeymoon phase
- ○ Rest and Relaxation phase
- ○ Disenchantment phase
- ○ Retirement routine phase

The Honeymoon phase

Those reading this book in the first stages of retirement will probably recognise this as a time of great excitement and new experiences. We may be saying, 'This is great – why didn't I do it before?' During this time the euphoria results in us feeling as if we have just started a very long holiday – long may that feeling last! The *honeymoon phase* typically lasts anywhere from a couple of months to one year, from the start of retirement, because it takes most people about 12 months to work through the range of activities we were looking forward to doing when we retired.

We may decide to read all the books on our 'to do' list; research and buy a new car; learn a new language; go back to 'school'; go on the overseas trips that have been planned for years; meet up with relatives and old friends; take on more grand-parenting responsibilities; decorate or renovate the house; have a good 'tidy up'; look for a new house; move to a new location; or organise a workshop or hobby room within the house.

During this busy time we are out of any normal routine and the realities of retirement may have not yet set in.

Rest and Relaxation Phase

In comparison with the honeymoon period this *rest and relaxation phase* is much lower key and for the happy retiree will take on the feel of a long leisurely holiday. For some, this phase may last forever because this is exactly how we want to spend our retirement. For those around us who had expectations of their recently retired partner, family member or friend 'doing things' it can be a disappointing time. However, it will not end until we are tired of relaxing, bored with doing very little, and begin to look for something else to do, perhaps with more meaning and purpose

Disenchantment Phase

It is important to recognise that some of us become disenchanted with our retirement, particularly if we have not thought much beyond those immediate treats, rewards, and adventures. It may not be until all our 'honeymoon' projects are completed that it dawns on us that the retirement years have now started. This realisation of reality can signal the end of the honeymoon period and it is then not unusual for us to enter periods of disappointment and even depression, anxiety or stress. This can be a puzzling and scary experience for those of us who were anticipating a carefree existence.

There is considerable evidence to suggest that the intensity and duration of the honeymoon phase is linked to the level of satisfaction experienced in pre-retirement work life. If we found our work boring or were unhappy, then retirement is more likely to be based on the need to escape rather than on the transition to life in retirement. This can make the onset of emotional problems such as depression doubly disturbing for those who had looked forward to many years of life in retirement and could lead to those people needing some medical help.

This disenchantment phase is similar to that felt in the pre-retirement phase outlined earlier in the chapter during the acknowledgement and acceptance phase, when we suddenly feel groundless and rootless, having a foot in each of two worlds, but not fitting into either. The future is unknown and we no longer fit into our past working life.

Some of us may have taken the time to plan and create our pre-retirement vision. However, it may have turned out to be rather unrealistic, too expensive, or not what we thought we really wanted to do at all. This can result in a feeling of emptiness. We started off retirement saying 'This is great – why didn't I do it before?' and we are now saying 'If only I knew what I really wanted...' There is further discussion on this later in the book.

Retirement routine phase

This is the good news phase. If our retirement has been based on thoughtful choices and sound decisions this should be a happy and contented time of stability when we have really settled into and accepted our new identity and routine. It is certainly not a boring phase as we will have at our fingertips the tools to re-kindle old passions, explore wider horizons, discover new opportunities and meet new challenges – or just take the time to appreciate and enjoy what we have already.

> '*The years go by, as quickly as a wink, enjoy yourself,*
> *enjoy yourself, it's later than you think...*'
>
> (Maxine Sullivan Listen, Appearance,
> Song Review All Music 2.10.1978)

It is therefore timely that the next chapter will consider one of the most common fears we have about retirement 'How will I spend my time?' and explore our personal relationship with time.

3

TIME
How Will I Spend
My Time?

FACTS

- Leisure and time use: Over sixty-fives spend on average three and three quarter hours a day watching TV (or DVD/video)
- Over-sixty-fives spend on average 80% of their time in the home – this rises to 90% for people over eighty-five

Later Life in the United Kingdom – Age UK – May 2015

From an early age we may have been taught that 'good things come to those who wait'. Some of us may have allowed future concerns to dominate our lives:

- When I start school I will…
- When I leave school I will…
- When I grow up I will…
- When I find the love of my life I will…
- When I get to the top of my career I will…
- When I have saved up enough for a deposit on a mortgage I will…
- When the children leave home I will…
- When I retire I will…

....

PAUSE FOR THOUGHT

– *Which good things in your life do you feel were worth waiting for?*

....

It can be quite a shock when we wake up one day and remember that this is that first glorious Monday morning of our retirement. The prospect of forty empty hours each week stretches before us forever, to do with as we wish. Throughout our life while we were building a career, adjusting to marriage, and raising a family, we may have dreamed about this day and having all this time to ourselves. This is the first week of a new adventure that promises free time and the enjoyment and satisfaction that go with it.

It is natural to feel resistance at first to this change in our lives and it can take a while to shake off the feeling that 'we should be doing this', and 'we should be doing that'. We no longer have to look over our shoulder as there is no one around to whom we have to account for our time. Suddenly we are in charge of structuring our day and deciding how we spend our time. This includes the things we no longer have to do as well as the things we want to do. If we want a change, then it is up to us to appreciate, and then act on, the new opportunities being offered to us so we can avoid the danger of our new free time being frittered away, or of losing control as it becomes structured by others. With a little planning, every Monday could become our Monday Moment, memorable in some small way, so that our retirement week starts off feeling very different from our working week and our todays look different from our yesterdays.

It is interesting to consider that we all have the same amount of time, yet we all spend it differently and we never have enough. Time can both be the most valuable and yet the most perishable of our possessions. If our time really is our own then it can be considered our only true personal asset.

'What, then is time?' asks St Augustine in his *Confessions* in AD 397 'If no one asks me, I know what it is. If I wish to explain it to him who asks me, I do not know. Yet I say with confidence that I know that if nothing passes away, there would be no past time; and if nothing were still coming, there would be no future time; and if there were nothing at all, there would be no present time.'

We talk about time as though it has a separate personality of its own. Time can be spent, time can be raced against, time can be filled, time can be marked, time can be saved, time can be measured, time can be wasted, time can be bought, and we can lose track of time. Time flies, time drags, time passes, time lies heavily, and time is precious.

In this chapter we will consider three writers and their perspectives on time that can help us to explore our own relationship with it; the impact it might have had on our lives; and insights into our use of time in retirement. These are:

- ○ *The Power of Now* – Eckhart Tolle
- ○ *Time Paradox* – Philip Zimbardo
- ○ *Mindfulness* – Jon Kabat-Zinnabat-Zinn

The Power of Now

In the *Power of Now* Eckhart Tolle states that: '…Time isn't precious at all, because it is an illusion. What you perceive as precious is not time but the one point that is out of time: the Now… nothing ever happens in the past; it happened in the Now. Nothing will ever happen in the future; it will happen in the Now.' *(Reprinted with permission of Hodder and Stoughton Limited and New World Library)*

Retirement can be seen as that life phase when, paradoxically, we have both the most time and the least time available to us. On retirement many of us are at our richest in terms of wealth, relationships, life experience and time. Therefore retirement gives us an opportunity to explore any long-held relationships we may have with time that might impact on our chances of a successful retirement.

Retirement is that time when we can stop doing things that we are doing now as a means to an end and bring the end nearer. Retirement is that time when we can stop trying to get somewhere other than where we are, and be where we want to be. Retirement is that time when we can stop waiting for the next celebration, the next anniversary, the next reunion, the next family visit, and enjoy each day.

PAUSE FOR THOUGHT

- *Is there anything you are still waiting for?*
- *Will retiring bring it nearer?*

If we are not living in the present, there is a danger that time will pass us by without us noticing. Although this is so throughout our lives, it becomes particularly important during our retirement to acknowledge our today, our now, our present, because if there is a tomorrow, it is a gift.

On retirement our life changes and we may also need to make some changes to adjust. It is not always, however, easy just to stop thinking about and living in the past, or to stop looking forward to and living for the future, and simply being in the present.

Time Paradox

In *Time Paradox,* Philip Zimbardo provides insights into how we can use what we have learned about the way we have spent our time in the past to inform our choices for our future 'present'.

From his research Zimbardo explains that we each have a perspective on time that reflects our attitudes, beliefs and values to time, and can impact on our thoughts, feelings and behaviours. When we think about our past, present and future 'our thoughts might be positive or negative, happy or sad, hopeful or fearful'. Thus it is important to explore our perspective on time, and the extent to which this might be contributing to our concerns or fears about retirement, and consequently may have a negative or positive impact on its success. The Time Paradox time perspectives considered here are:

- ○ Past positive perspective
- ○ Past negative perspective
- ○ Present hedonistic perspective
- ○ Present fatalistic perspective
- ○ Future oriented perspective

Past positive time perspective

What we believe happened in the past can influence our present thoughts, feelings and behaviour more than what did actually happen. Someone who takes this perspective on time has a positive attitude to the past regardless of whether events that occurred in the past were actually good or bad. The event may well have been positive, or it could be that our positive attitude has helped us to look back and make the best out of the situation. Zimbardo's research shows that those of us who are able to recall our difficult past experiences in a positive way tend to be happier, more resilient and optimistic individuals.

If we are fortunate to have a past positive perspective then it is something we should take with us into our retirement and consciously maintain when any difficulties occur. It is worth mentioning here that our Time perspective can also have an effect on our attitude to money. Pasts tend to learn from the past and therefore any future investments will be designed to conserve money or avoid losing money, rather than making more of it.

If we start to take a positive attitude to the future, and acknowledge that the future, for which we have been planning so conscientiously is now our present, then it is more likely that we will enjoy our retirement years.

Past negative time perspective

The past negative time perspective also reflects our attitude to events that occurred in the past. Negative attitudes may be due to the actual experience of negative events or to the negative interpretation that we have chosen to bring to those events. While it is not possible to change the events themselves, it is possible for us to change our thoughts, feelings and behaviours towards them.

Retirement provides a good opportunity to leave behind some of this negativity as some of the concerns and fears that we might have about retirement could be tied up with our perspective on the past. It is a good time to re-examine our attitudes, beliefs and values in relation to time and the impact this might be having on our activities and relationships. It also provides the opportunity for a different daily routine and this is a good time to make personal modifications in our lives. Just because the past has had an influence over our lives it does not need to continue to control our future. Certain situations may not have gone the way we wanted them to during our life but that is the past and that is history. Those who follow Positive Psychology take the view that the effect of situations to influence our present and our future is only powerful if we allow it to be so.

Present hedonistic time perspective

Present hedonists actively seek pleasure and try to avoid anything in life that might give pain. Those of us with this time perspective will have focused on the immediate and may not be one of those people who believes that 'good things come to those who wait'. We can be great company and fun to be around, but we also have a tendency to drop activities and those around us, once they become tedious or boring. We use our money to create fun and excitement now, with little consideration for the past or the future.

If this has been our overriding attitude to life then it is possible we might be concerned that in retirement, without the contrast of a work schedule, and the necessary tedium of having to earn a living, there will be fewer opportunities for fun and excitement. In terms of attitude towards money the Present hedonist is likely to have been attracted by get-rich-quick schemes and may not always be as financially prepared for retirement as other perspectives.

Present fatalist time perspective

This time perspective is taken by those of us who believe that nothing we do can make a difference to our future. This may be because we believe that we were not given the same opportunities during childhood and through education as those around us. It could be that everything we have tried has not produced the desired results.

We were not born unhappy and therefore, if this is a perspective we do not want to take with us into retirement, it is a good time to work on converting some of the negatives in our lives into positives.

Future oriented time perspective

In the same way as no one is born unhappy, no one is born with a future time perspective. We become future oriented over time through the positive influence of those around us. We may have been influenced by parents, teachers, friends, and those we choose to listen to in the media. Futures work hard, plan ahead, recognise any obstacles that might appear, achieve goals and can problem solve their way out of situations. Futures can end up making more money than people with other time perspectives, because they are less likely to fritter money away on socialising or get-rich-quick schemes. Futures will be best prepared for retirement because they have organised their lives around plans, goal achievement and problem solving.

The challenge for Futures in retirement is the realisation that the bright future, or the rainy day, for which they have been planning all their life, is now here, and ready to be enjoyed. Learning to live in the present and practising a little hedonism could improve the enjoyment Futures gain from their retirement.

In Time Paradox we are reassured that time gives us three paths to happiness. These are the past, the present and the future. However we are advised that the wise will take advantage of all three to give balance. 'We can learn from our past; we can be guided by a clear vision and plan for our future; but we can only make changes and live our life in the present'. *(Reprinted with permission of Atria Books, a Division of Simon & Schuster, Inc.)*

If we spend too much time thinking about, and living in the past, or looking forward and living for the future, then we are not living in the present. In the view of Zimbardo, we can only think, feel and do in the present. When we think about the past we are thinking about it in the present and re-living our memories. When we think about the future we are thinking about it in the present but the future is in our imagination until it becomes our present. In the view of Eckhart Tolle the past and future have no reality of their own. They are borrowed from the present. The example given is that of the moon and the sun. 'The moon has no light of its own but reflects the light from the sun'.

During retirement the present becomes really important. We cannot ignore the past, and we cannot stop planning for the future, but this is the time to recognise that we are living our life in this moment. It is easier to control our enjoyment and happiness in this moment, in this present. To live in the present means to focus and be aware of the present. We stop worrying about what has happened in the past and what might happen in the future. As we get older and we are having conversations with those we have known for a long time it is tempting to delve back to the past rather than keeping our attention on the present. When we are talking to a younger generation it is tempting to go over what we used to do or think rather than being curious and trying to understand their current ideas.

PAUSE FOR THOUGHT
- *Do you consider that the way you have used your time in the past has been influenced by any of these perspectives?*
- *Do you want these perspectives to continue to influence what you do in your retirement?*
- *What would you want to do differently?*

Mindfulness

A popular approach to living in the present, or The Now, is Mindfulness. Jon Kabat-Zinn was considered the founder of Mindfulness. He was first introduced to meditation by Philip Kapleau, a Zen missionary who went to speak at MIT(Massachusetts Institute of Technology) when Kabat-Zinn was a student. He studied meditation with other Buddhist teachers and by adapting the Buddhist teachings on mindfulness developed his Stress Reduction and Relaxation programme. He removed the Buddhist framework and it was renamed Mindfulness.

The practice of Mindfulness involves 'paying attention on purpose, and in a particular non-judgmental way, to the present moment'. Again this practice recognises that our lives unfold in moments, and if we are always busy thinking and doing, and we are not consciously paying attention to those moments, then we fail to appreciate any feelings of happiness and enjoyment.

In his book *Mindfulness: A Practical Guide to Finding Peace in a Frantic World* Professor Mark Williams explains that it operates on two levels. First is the core mindfulness meditation programme consisting of a series of simple daily meditations. Second, it encourages the breaking of some of the unconscious habits of thinking and behaving that stops us from living life to the full. His book sets out an eight week Mindfulness programme.

If time is an illusion then it is comforting for us to think that it is never too late. We may have procrastinated in the past about things we want to do, but the forty extra hours a week we have been given in retirement provides us with that special gift of a second chance.

No matter what we claim our expectations or our dreams might be, our real expectations, dreams and values are expressed by how we spend our time. When things are important to us we find a way to fit them in.

Successful retirement requires a retirement activity plan that includes the things we no longer have to do, as well as the things we want to do. When we have decided how we want to spend our time then this will help us in our financial planning, and as far as we are able, the emphasis we place on our well-being. After a life of working we have earned the personal asset that is our 'free' time and it is now up to us how we use it well.

....

PAUSE FOR THOUGHT

- *What changes to your use of time would you like to make in retirement?*
- *What would you like to stop doing?*
- *What would be the consequences?*
- *How will you overcome any obstacles?*
- *What would you like to do more of?*
- *What would be the consequences?*
- *How will you overcome any obstacles?*
- *What is not on your list that you would like to do?*

....

Time is not our only personal asset. As we will see in the next chapter we also have our personality, strengths, talents, values and motivations that make up our identity. Our values and motivations will be considered in later chapters.

4

IDENTITY

Who Will I Become When I Am Retired? Losing, Leaving, Letting Go and Moving On

FACTS

○ 60% of older people in the UK agree that age discrimination exists in the daily lives of older people
○ 53% of adults agree that once you reach very old age, people tend to treat you as a child

Later Life in the United Kingdom – Age UK – May 2015

Our identity is the sum of the roles we play. It is what we have done, what we do, how we see ourselves, how we see the world, the inner life we live and the outer life we lead. We are a mixture of our personality, strengths, talents, and values reflected in our own self-concept of who we are. We also have a number of identities. Each time we meet someone, although there may be only two people in the room, there are at least six identities exposed in that room. These are the identity of the person we each think we are, our own self-concept; the identity of the person we each think the other is, our perception of the other; and the identity of the person we each think the other thinks we are, our perception of the other's perception.

PAUSE FOR THOUGHT

– *Who am I?* Write down 10 facts about yourself. You may wish to ask someone close to you to help you

Although we have a number of identities, for many of us our career identity is the one that has the most visibility, is the most public and probably drives our view of ourselves. It is also the role to which we most have to conform and that we spend most of our time playing.

Once we leave our career behind we are free to explore our other identities. We may lose our career identity when we leave work, but this gives us the opportunity to find a new identity and take the opportunity to be that person we always wanted to be when we grew up. We now have time to make the most of our strengths and talents and write our book, learn that language, change our style, be better grandparents, and resolve unresolved conflicts.

Retirement is a time of unlimited possibilities and the right time to be asking ourselves 'Who am I?' 'Who am I now that I am retiring?' 'How do I want to be introduced in my retirement years?' 'When are we officially considered a grown up?' 'Is retirement a natural passage between adulthood and grownuphood?' If so, 'Am I that person I always wanted to be when I grew up?'

If not, then in *Revitalising Retirement* Nancy J Schlossberg recommends 'now is the time for me to renew my relationship with that person I wanted to be and find out if we have a future together'. There are many starting points for self-discovery and self-awareness to help us with the question 'Who am I?'

One of the most simplistic but popular is the personality classifications recognised by the Myers-Briggs model as personality preferences.

So Who Am I Now? Personality

It is likely that we have chosen the type of work we do and our working environment to fit in with our personality preferences. Recognising the contribution our preferences play in our own sense of satisfaction will be important when choosing our retirement activities.

This means that we are quite capable of accessing our less preferred personality dimensions and are not locked into always behaving in the same way. Retirement provides us with the opportunity to challenge our personality preferences and experiment with others along the scale. There are four sub scales that classify our personality and help us to recognise our personalities.

....

PAUSE FOR THOUGHT

- *As you read through the next section can you recognise any of these personality preferences in yourself or others?*
- *Do you think it is necessary for your retirement activities to replicate your working environment or is this the time to do things differently?*

....

Extraversion (E) which is the opposite of Introversion (I)
Extraverts prefer tasks involving interactions with people and Introverts will often prefer tasks where they can quietly focus. During retirement extraverts will continue to need stimulation, challenge and groups of people around them. Introverts prefer to communicate on a one to one basis or in small groups they know well. If they want to replicate this in retirement then it will be necessary to work on creating and building up these small groups before retirement.

Sensing (S) which is the opposite of Intuition (N)
Sensing is the way we prefer to take in information from the world around us. We may see things by applying our five senses or we may prefer to look for possibilities and meaning by focusing more on the bigger picture. Those with a Sensing preference are more likely to rely on past experience as their most highly valued basis for arriving at decisions. They will require activities in retirement that are practical, measurable, observable and have outcomes.

Intuitives tend to look more for what possibilities the future holds for them and look forward to change and to events in the future. They get pleasure from acquiring new skills and knowledge and in solving new and complex problems. By using their imagination and insight they will often act as a catalyst for constructive discussion among other members of a group. Work may have provided them with a natural outlet for their preferences which they may need to replicate for a satisfying retirement.

Thinking (T) which is the opposite of Feeling (F)

The ways those with a thinking preference arrive at decisions are more likely to rely on objective logic and will be influenced mostly by facts. Thinking preferences may be more comfortable in roles where they need to apply logic rather than dealing with the emotional problems of others; roles where they can be tough minded and useful for financial decisions that require an analytical solution. There may be less opportunity to demonstrate this preference outside the work environment and they may therefore find aspects of retirement frustrating.

Those with Feeling preferences will be influenced by values rather than by the logical outcome and will prefer to make decisions where the outcomes do not affect others adversely. Feelings tend to display their emotions more openly and enjoy pleasing others. In retirement there may be opportunities to display this preference within areas such as voluntary work where caring is integral to the role.

Judging (J) which is the opposite of Perceiving (P)

Those with Judging preferences are keen to act on decisions as soon as possible with a high need for closure. Judging preferences enjoy activities that involve a reasonably high level of structure. Once a plan of action is decided, changes to the original plan are disliked. This may require some tolerance by others within the retirement environment.

Perceptives, on the other hand, may feel pressured by a tight deadline, arguing that more time is needed to gather more information before action, just in case there is some important issue that has not yet been considered. Perceptives will most likely enjoy activities involving change or flexibility from rigid schedules. Where it is important that an activity or project is complete on time, Perceptives need to be careful that they do not keep postponing the completion of tasks because they need more information. Perceptives will not enjoy too much routine and repetition in retirement.

So Who Am I Now? Strengths and Talents

PAUSE FOR THOUGHT (ask others to help)
- *My strengths are...*
- *The talents I naturally give to others are...*
- *The talents I most enjoy giving to others are...*

So Who Am I Now That I Am Retiring ?

Initially, when we go through the process of disengaging from our workplace, we may find ourselves travelling on an emotional rollercoaster. It is exciting to recognise that we may be exiting from a well-worn and comfortable identity into something completely new and unknown. However, it can also be a stressful time. If we are forewarned it allows us to openly discuss the process with others before it happens, anticipate the challenges and emotions we may encounter, and seek advice, rather than muddling our way through. If we have not done so already we can use these insights as a motivation to start to build ourselves a bridge between the loss of our old identity and the discovery of our new identity, the loss of our old working life and the replacement by our new liberated life, that we call retirement.

When we think of loss we tend to think of the loss, through death, of people we love. As Judith Viorst states in *Necessary Losses* '…loss is a far more encompassing theme in our life. For we lose not only through death, but also by leaving and being left, by changing and letting go and moving on.'

When we think back over our lives we will have already recovered from a number of losses by rebuilding aspects of our life. We will have had to recover from losses associated with the unmet promises of our youth; our younger self; past loves; unfulfilled dreams; trust in relationships; marriages; unachieved career goals; our sense of security; wasted investment in our passions; good health and well-being; and the sense that our lives will last forever. During the transition from work to retirement it can be helpful to look back at those losses and the way we dealt with them in the past. It is possible that we grew stronger and developed as a person through the transition process of losing, leaving, letting go and moving on.

PAUSE FOR THOUGHT

- *Have any previous losses in your life impacted on your identity?*
- *How did you recover from your changing circumstances?*
- *Can you draw on the personal resources you used at that time to help during this transition to re-shape your identity?*

Leaving behind our Career Identity

'What do you do?' is usually the first question we are asked when we meet someone new. Our job title and job description help us to describe to strangers immediately who we are and what we do. Each job has its own particular status attached to it. It can take time for us to feel comfortable about not being identified primarily by our career identity. This is particularly so for those of us who have enjoyed our work and for whom work has given us a certain status, sense of personal value, and self-esteem. When we finally leave work and retire we are not only leaving and losing a place to which to go each morning, we are also leaving and losing behind an identity, a group of colleagues to connect with, the satisfaction of a task achieved at the end of the day, confirmation of our competence, and a salary that puts a value on that competence.

It is inevitable that leaving the familiarity of possibly decades and moving into the unknown can contribute to our feeling of a loss of worth and self-esteem. Therefore, losing our career identity and having to find a new one is one of the greatest fears facing us when we retire.

Some individuals find it harder to shake off their career identity than others. We can often hang on to it at the expense of developing a new identity, particularly if we are unhappy or dissatisfied with our retirement lives. This can sometimes turn into a feeling of nostalgia. While this can be helpful in a past positive way there is also a danger that we only recall pleasurable events and push aside any negative experiences. Eventually this can then become boring and tedious to those around us who may perceive things differently.

Individuals leaving professional and semi-professional roles tend to find it more difficult than individuals leaving non-professional roles. In the process of becoming a 'professional' changes occur in the self-identity of a person as they internalise their professional role and define themselves in terms of the role expectations. Often an individual is attracted to the high idealism attached to that role from an early age and will have undertaken a long training and induction process. Roles in the law, accountancy, police, Church, medical and other professions are highly visible in society and tend to be roles that are very difficult to leave behind completely on retirement.

In the past this has been a bigger problem for men rather than women. Work has been psychologically different for men than for women. Women have had the advantage at retirement of the continuity of their role and identity within the home and the family. However, now that women are spending as long as men in the workplace and creating their own career identity this psychological difference is narrowing and women too are faced with how to replace it. The danger for women is that having worked for nearly half a century managing a career, home and family, it will be difficult, when we retire, to resist the expectations of family and government to take on the multiple roles of elder care, spouse care, adult child care, and grandchild care. Such a temptation needs to be balanced with a sense of entitlement to pursue our own personal passions and dreams.

Reshaping the identity we share with work colleagues

One of the obvious but significant changes in the life of a retiree is the changed relationship with work colleagues, who may have become friends. Once we leave the group with which we have established a shared identity and shared purpose in the workplace it is a challenge to navigate a new relationship that still has some value for each of us. We may continue to meet up but we gradually realise that we no longer have any nuggets of information to exchange, shared concerns to discuss, and current opinions to contribute. Then the emails and the phone calls stop coming. The friendships can last but the basis on which they continue will have changed and the retiree is the one who will have to work hard to remain of value.

Replacing our norm reference group

If we have worked in an organisation for a long time, when we retire we suddenly realise that the expectations we have of ourselves and others have of us; the norms that we have taken for granted; the framework within which we are used to making decisions; and the identity by which we have recognised ourselves and others recognise us, all change. The way we measured our performance and our success in the past no longer exist in our new world. Therefore we have to navigate differently, establish new benchmarks and new reference groups against which to judge our success.

Re-inventing ourselves in the eyes of others

We have to learn to deal with the reaction of other people in relation to who we used to be. We may now be treated differently, possibly not very kindly or not with the same respect, from the way we have been in the past. Our value to others may diminish or vanish altogether. The way we present ourselves to the new world of retirement will determine how we will now be treated.

Re-inventing ourselves before our own eyes

When we leave work our dress style and our image will change. Even if we have not needed to wear a uniform, we may well have dressed in a certain way to fit in with the type of work we do, our colleagues and our role. When we have shopped for clothes for work we have probably not had to give our choices much thought. We may have had work clothes, formal casual, informal casual and then clothes for special occasions. Retirement provides an exciting opportunity for both men and women to take some professional advice on our re-styling and re-imaging. This may coincide with a renewed enthusiasm for some weight loss and exercise (Chapter 10) and the thought of a new wardrobe and a new image can provide added motivation. This will contribute to our new identity and our decisions about how we want to present ourselves to the world. It will also encourage those around us to see us differently. This is just as important for a man as it is for a woman.

Re-establishing our personal friendship groups

At the same time as we are adjusting to changes to our relationships with our work colleagues, changes can also occur in our personal friendship groups. Some of our friends, and those we value, may have already retired and have no space in their life for a newly energised retiree; other friends have not retired and still have no space in their life for a newly energised retiree; and some of our friendships may not necessarily flourish if we spend more time together.

Restoring our self-esteem

Self-esteem can be described as the sum of our levels of self-respect and self-acceptance. Self-esteem affects the way we behave, think and feel. When we have a high level of self-esteem we tend to have a high level of self-respect. In his book *The Beginner's Guide to Retirement,* Michael Longhurst states that our level of self-esteem depends on our self-concept. Our self-concept was shaped by the influences of the adults in our life when our personality was developing. Our self-worth and self-concept was influenced by the quality and consistency of the positive feedback they provided.

If our self-esteem has been built up through our work but we have not allowed it to flourish in other areas of our lives, then retirement is the time to pay attention to our family, friends, leisure interests and passions. Feelings of low self-esteem often build up over a lifetime, and letting go of ingrained feelings and behaviours is not an easy task. It may take time, hard work, and it may require professional help. But there are some simple, positive thinking techniques used in Positive Psychology that can be used to help improve self-esteem. These are called affirmations. Affirmations are encouraging messages we can give ourselves every day until they become part of our feelings and beliefs. Using affirmations to stop negative self-talk is considered by some professionals as a simple, positive way to help increase self-esteem.

PAUSE FOR THOUGHT
- *How did you introduce yourself to a stranger 10 years ago?*
- *How do you introduce yourself to a stranger now?*
- *How would you like to be able to introduce yourself to a stranger in five years' time.*

As we have seen in this chapter, when we lose our career identity it can have a significant impact on our relationships at work and our self-esteem. How we deal with this change determines how we will be treated by others. The next chapter focuses on how our relationships can change when we retire.

5

RELATIONSHIPS
How Will My
Relationships Change?

FACTS

- Loneliness can be as harmful for our health as smoking 15 cigarettes a day
- People with a high degree of loneliness are twice as likely to develop Alzheimer's than people with a low degree of loneliness
- 49% of over sixty-fives in UK say that television or pets are their main form of company
- 37% of over sixty-fives consider the television as their main form of company
- 12% of over sixty-fives say their pets are their main form of company
- 17% of older people have less than weekly contact with family, friends and neighbours and 11% have less than monthly contact

Later Life in the United Kingdom – Age UK – May 2015

Leaving the world of work behind often causes retirees to re-examine every area of their lives. When one person retires the entire family is affected. We can go from having no time on our hands during the years when time is at a premium, balancing work and family and friendships, to having too much time on our hands if we do not have enough to do in retirement. Suddenly, retirement gives us more time to spend with partners, children, family and friends, but this change does not always run smoothly. As we learned earlier, before we retire we should have an open and honest conversation with everyone who will share our retirement and exchange our expectations. This is the opportunity to explore and understand everyone's ideas about our relationships in retirement, particularly the needs of partners and children.

Robert Weiss in *The Provisions of social relationships* found that relationships can be categorised by the benefits they provide, and as a consequence, we have a need to maintain or establish a number of different relationships for our wellbeing. When we leave work we can lose certain relationships that have provided some of these benefits. If we recognise this before we retire we can start to replace these benefits by establishing new relationships or re-connecting with existing relationships. The benefits we gain from working relationships are:

○ **Reassurance of our worth** when our competence is affirmed by relationships within our family, community or work. Work provided us with this sense of achievement of a day well spent, formal and informal feedback, annual appraisals, and our salary as the ultimate recognition of our value. Partners of retirees may need to acknowledge this loss and recognise that it may be necessary to provide more re-assurance within the relationship. Alternatively this sense of worth and self-esteem can be replaced through volunteering or part-time work.

○ **Guidance and advice** we receive through relationships where the other person has been trusted over time to provide good counsel and advice when we need it. We may have had mentors or colleagues at work whose wisdom extended beyond the workplace and whose judgement we trusted on out-of-work issues. We may not appreciate the value of these relationships until we no longer have ready access to them. When we retire we may have to start to look elsewhere for that guidance and build up new contacts through a process of trial and error.

○ **Personal growth** through relationships that are intellectually challenging. We all enjoy a good friendly argument with colleagues, family members and friends whose opinions we respect. In a healthy work environment this is likely to have been normal practice undertaken from a position of strength and security. When we retire we may no longer have easy access to intellectual stimulation and challenge. We might take up further study or a new interest that stretches us and requires brainwork. It will also be an opportunity to establish a new, interesting and diverse group of friends so that our personal growth continues.

○ **Our need for justifiable enemies** is served through the formal and informal relationships determined at work. Competitors, customers, departments other than our own, our boss or the management all meet our need of 'enemyship'. Research undertaken by Mark J Landau in *An*

Existential Function of Enemyship: Evidence That People Attribute Influence to Personal and Political Enemies to Compensate for Threats to Control established that enemies serve a function and a need in human beings. We like to perceive ourselves as controlling our environment yet we realise that our lives can often be negatively affected by a number of outside factors. To minimise this threat we tend to narrow down our misfortune to a particular individual or group that can be effectively controlled, managed or at least understood. The 'enemy' can then be blamed for any misfortune that befalls us and allows us to maintain a sense of personal control and a sense that risk is less randomly distributed. When we retire the danger is that we no longer have these 'justifiable enemies' to blame for our misfortunes and will therefore transfer the blame for any misfortunes to those nearest to us.

....

PAUSE FOR THOUGHT

- *Can you recognise who (if anyone) within your work circle provided the benefits described above?*
- *Will you need to find replacements for these relationships when you retire?*
- *If so, how will you do this?*

....

As we get older it is possible to feel that time is passing more quickly and something begins to change in our relationships during the second half of our life. Our values may start to move from career success and materialism to finding meaning and purpose to our lives, and the quality of our relationships becomes more important. These are the benefits we gain from other relationships we nurture outside of work:

- **Attachment and reliable alliance** is provided by relationships that are constant and safe, such as our partnership, family and close friends.

- **Social integration** is provided through relationships in which the individuals have similar concerns to our own. This usually occurs when people work together towards a common goal and can include self-help groups, interest groups, charity work, local community committees. As work may have satisfied this need many retirees find it satisfying to substitute volunteer work for paid work.

- **Being nurtured and to nurture** through relationships in which we care for friends, family and children. This gives us meaning and purpose and helps us feel that we matter because we are needed. The danger is that when the nurturing comes to an end we may feel a great loss of purpose once again if it is the main focus of our retirement activity. This may follow the death of our parents or when the grandchildren go off to school. It is important, therefore, to ensure that we do not replace work with too much nurturing of others and there is no time for nurturing of ourselves.

○ **Protection against loneliness** and the opportunity to stay connected to the outside world which helps to increase our sense of well-being.

○ **Enjoyment and fun** is served, hopefully, through all our relationships. They would be sad relationships if they did not provide us with life positives. However, retirement might be a good time to review all our relationships to see if it is time to let any of them go. If some of our relationships are a drain then we need to ask ourselves for whose benefit we are continuing with them. One of the recommendations from Positive Psychology is to surround ourselves with positive people. (Chapter 6)

....

PAUSE FOR THOUGHT
Choose 4 people who are important in your life

1.

2.

3.

4.

- *Which relationships feel most supportive?*
- *What contribution do you make to those relationships?*
- *Are there any relationships that are in need of work?*
- *Who could put in the work?*

....

Relationship changes at work and around work

When we retire we will almost certainly have considered how we will replace our salary cheque and will have built up our financial capital, but few of us will have considered what sociologists and economists refer to as our 'social capital'. This is the network of relationships we derive from our work. Our financial capital provides us with security for the future and hopefully will generate income for our retirement. Social capital is similar, being our ties at work, with our colleagues and our intellectual community.

For most people work provides a physical place to go most days and regular contact with others. Even people who work at home usually have a routine that brings them into contact with others. However this routine disappears when we retire and our world of work goes quiet. Former colleagues begin to lose interest in us. We may expect our professional relationships to continue when we retire but after a while the phone does not ring and the emails stop coming. We no longer share the same life cycle and are out of the loop. Work friendships remain cordial but distant. If we meet up we find ourselves focusing on the old issues, topics relating to our last work together. However these are no longer current and no longer relevant to our former colleagues and they have moved on.

Our shared values and interests were the work itself; working as a team on tasks and challenges with our peers; observing the way we were performing; undertaking morale boosting activities; and organisational gossip. Once we leave an organisation we also leave its values, and as time passes we recognise that we are no longer part of what we were, and the motivation on both sides to keep in regular contact with former work colleagues decreases.

If we have not done so before we left work, we need to put effort into extending our existing positive relationships or establish a new friendship retirement-relevant group. There will be no one else to keep up our morale other than ourselves.

While we are working it is not only in our actual place of work that we form relationships. If we do not live near our work we also make contacts in the wider locality. The long-lasting relationships we had struck over the years with the local-to-work dry cleaners, florists, coffee shop owner, or petrol station attendant, who knew our personal preferences and tastes better than we did, are no longer on our daily doorstep. We will never now know the twists and turns of their own lives and the endings of their stories. We will also have to negotiate with a new set of services and start to develop meaningful relationships within our new locality, our new routine and our new activities.

When we stop working we change our routine. If we went to the gym or exercise classes before or after work and change the times of our visits, then the experience no longer feels familiar. The casual acquaintances we were on nodding terms with, and we took for granted would always be part of the experience, are no longer there at that time.

We no longer have to make our journey to and from work. That means that we no longer see the familiar sunrise and sunset, the occasional rainbow over the hills, and the changing seasons of the same landscape. If we want to continue our easy and natural relationship with nature and the outdoors then more effort is required and it has to be found elsewhere.

Relationship changes with our partner

For couples who retire, either separately or together, there are six identities in the course of change. In addition to our individual identity, we are re-visiting our relationship with each other as a retiree, and our new relationship as a retired couple

At the start of this chapter we stated that leaving the world of work behind often causes retirees to re-examine every area of their lives. Probably the relationship that is affected the most when we retire is our relationship with our partner. Sometimes spending more time together does not work as smoothly as we both expected.

For couples retirement is often a major change in the relationship and the thought of spending more time, maybe all day and every day together, can be a real concern. Negotiating space, time, boundaries and dreams can be a big issue if you have not spent a lot of time together over the years. If you are in a couple, *The Couple's Retirement Puzzle* by Roberta K. Taylor and Dorian Mintzer provides an excellent basis for all the essential conversations and Expectation Exchanges you should be having for 'your relationship not only to survive, but to thrive'.

Throughout our busy working life we have probably been consciously or unconsciously negotiating with each other to find a balance as an individual and as a couple between working, building a home, bringing up a family, and possibly pursuing our own interests. Often couples arrive at retirement having completed activities jointly and having built a life together, but grown apart without realising it. Similarly, our retirement preparations may have been separate as well as together. Therefore the earlier in the retirement preparation process the issue of when time will be spent alone, and when time will be spent together, is discussed and resolved, the less likely it will become a challenge to the success of both retirements.

Having an Expectations Exchange conversation, well before retirement, with a partner about what it will be like when more time is spent together is probably the most important conversation any of us will have about retirement. It is probably even more important than the conversation we will have with our financial adviser, although both conversations are obviously very much related.

When we have each other's undivided attention, when we are together all the time, the little things that both would have overlooked or did not have the time to notice in the past, become magnified because there might be little else to worry about in retirement.

However, there may be previously unresolved areas of disagreement that could prove disruptive and derail the possibility of a happy retirement spent together if no attempt is made early to resolve the potential conflict. One of these areas could relate to our differing views on how to approach our relationship with our parents, children and grandchildren now that we have more time in retirement.

Men and women can experience retirement differently. David Gutmann in *Reclaimed Powers: Men and Women in Later Life* suggests that older men and women experience a sex role reverse in retirement. Both men and women reclaim those aspects of their lives that may have remained dormant. A woman who may have spent her time raising a family may want to explore new horizons and choose to take on a major commitment outside the home. Men who were single-minded and assertive following through their career may become more nurturing and enjoy spending time with their grandchildren in a way they did not with their own children.

Often a couple will retire at different times and this brings its own challenges. The power balance in the relationship can change. One of the partners may have played second place to their partner's job and they may have relinquished their career earlier in life so that the children could be brought up. That partner may have then embarked on their own career later in life. When their partner retires they may not take kindly to being asked to set aside their newly acquired career to become a companion.

Conflict still arises when one partner willingly continues to work and be busy, while the retired partner is perceived as 'doing nothing all day', spending all day watching television, shopping, out with friends, reading, or fishing and doing what retired people do. When couples retire at different times it is even more crucial that the Expectations Exchange conversation takes place. As we saw in Chapter 4 we are changing both our individual identity and our identity as a couple.

Therefore, the satisfaction of our retirement could depend on the time and effort we put into the changes that occur in our relationship with our partner.

PAUSE FOR THOUGHT

You may wish to answer these questions separately as a couple and then together as part of your Expectations Exchange

- *Have you talked together about your timetable for retirement?*
- *Do you normally make financial and other life affecting decisions together?*
- *Have you discussed how your roles may change as you go through the transition from work to retirement?*
- *Have you discussed how you will arrange both 'time together' and 'time apart' during your retirement?*
- *Do you share the same values and understand what is important to each of you in your retirement?*

Relationship changes with our children and stepchildren

Carl Jung said, 'The most powerful influence on a child is the unlived life of the parent – or our own longings, missed opportunities, or losses, which have created emotional holes in our heart.' This can be taken in two ways. On the one hand it may be saying that parents often sacrifice living their own lives because they want to do the very best for their children. On the other hand it may be saying that parents have particular unfulfilled dreams of their own and wish to push their children down a direction they themselves wish they had taken. Retirement is a good time to take stock of our relationship with our adult children.

Retirement often empowers parents and step parents to look at our adult children in new ways and change the dynamics of the parent/child relationship. We can approach these changes in different ways.

Some parents want more involvement in the lives of their children and grandchildren now that they have no work to think about and have time on their hands. However, this can keep parents from having to make other more difficult decisions about what else to do with their time. They may decide to devote all their time and effort to the family because they do not know where else to put their efforts. Some parents hang on to their children because without their parental role they feel they have no other purpose.

This issue can cause conflict between couples who may have honest disagreement about parenting. It may always have been the case, but it is brought in greater focus on retirement. One may want more involvement with their children, while the other may want more separation and to spend time together as a couple. Ideally retired couples will find a balance where they have strong adult, mature, and loving relationships with their children. Partners can help each other achieve this by discussing situations that might affect that balance.

Many parents would really enjoy time alone with an adult child, but they are reluctant to ask for it. The son or daughter-in-law may be very nice indeed, but they are not your child. The grandchildren may be wonderful but you do not have forty years of history with them. If you take part in an Expectations Exchange conversation then you can ask for time together. If it happens naturally and easily from time to time a lot of hard feelings could be prevented.

At the other extreme some parents can be very selfish about their own needs. They may feel they have sacrificed enough when the children were young and now it is their time to do everything they can for themselves. On the other hand parents may have been driven away by recognising that their children are not grateful for what they have been given financially and emotionally and they themselves must take a break from this.

Some children are both financially and emotionally stable and have no reason to make demands on their parents. They are happy for their parents to have the retirement they want for themselves.

Others may feel they can call on their parents now for all kinds of help knowing it will be difficult for them to refuse. Parents may have more time but they may also have less money and their children may not believe them when they are told there will be fewer treats to meals out or for grandchildren's expenses.

Adult children may also have their own expectations about how their parents should live. Many children express concern that their parents would have time on their hands or perhaps become depressed. Others worry about the future cost of care and how it may eat into their parents' income and savings. Some feel rejected by their parents' involvement with retirement activities and resent their newly found freedom.

There are many retired couples who move to be near their adult children and grandchildren. For some adult children it is a relief to have extra help and support, for others it may feel like a burden and responsibility.

This is why the Expectations Exchange mentioned at the beginning of the chapter is so important.

....

PAUSE FOR THOUGHT
- *Have you yet embarked on your Expectations Exchange conversation with your children?*
- *Are your children aware of your plans for retirement?*
- *Do they understand the life positives and life challenges you see in your retirement?*
- *Have you discussed the changes that retirement might bring to your relationship with your children?*

....

Relationship changes with our grandchildren
When they arrive grandchildren have a special impact on our lives.

On retirement grandparents are in a better position to spend time with, buy things for, and give love to their grandchildren. It is likely that the birth of children to our own children changes our relationship with them and can often provide the opportunity to resolve troublesome issues.

However, with the number of couples working and the cost of childcare, increasingly grandparents are being expected to take on the majority of the grandchild care on a regular basis. Over time this restricts their own retirement activities and can become a source of disagreement between partners. Unless expectations are clearly set out over commitment and boundaries at the start of any arrangement there is the potential for problems between the grandparents and their children.

Sometimes grandparents sacrifice the early and active years of their retirement gaining a great deal of satisfaction from their grandchildren, only to find later that their grandchildren have less time for them when they get older and they themselves need some care.

Unfortunately, some grandparents have to take on the care of their grandchildren full-time if tragedy occurs or they gain custody because of neglect or abuse. In these circumstances there is no real retirement for them.

PAUSE FOR THOUGHT

- *Have you discussed with your children the importance your grandchildren play in your life?*
- *What expectations do they have of you as a retired grandparent?*
- *Have you discussed the changes that retirement might bring to your relationship with your grandchildren, both positive and negative?*

Relationship changes with our parents

If we know that there are others who depend on us financially, we tend to delay retirement as long as possible. However, sometimes we feel we would be better able to care for others if we gave up work and retired. In these circumstances our lives and retirement can be kept on hold. Each individual differs in the amount of responsibility they feel for others. Some of us care very much about the welfare of others, while others are able to feel disinterested or deny completely the needs of others. Retirement is supposed to be a time for fulfilling our own hopes and dreams but in more and more cases care-giving takes over our lives. This is not only the case if we have elderly relatives but if we have children or siblings that also need continued care.

As we are all living longer and the social care available in the community is reducing, more and more of us have to decide how much of ourselves we should be devoting to care-giving and for how long. Dr Richard P Johnson in *What Color Is Your Retirement?* advises us 'to draw up care-giving boundaries setting out limits in the amount, intensity, and breadth of the care-giving we are capable of giving'. It is when the boundaries have not been clear from the outset through the Expectations Exchange conversations that frustrations on both sides can occur. It is therefore important to do this as early as possible in retirement before misunderstandings can occur.

In his view it is common for caregivers to overestimate the needs of their aging parent, or overestimate the amount of care they can provide without becoming ill themselves. It is also possible to overestimate the amount of care required by the elderly. 'There is a difference between becoming care managers and being the sole care-giver'. Care-givers need to ensure that they look after themselves, and take advantage of all the support that is available, so that they too can have some fun and enjoyment during their retirement without feeling guilty.

While we are spending our time caring for others it is important to consider who will take care of us when that time comes, and what living options will be open to us. (Chapter 9)

The care of parents can sometimes cause friction within partnerships. Some people are happy to care for their own parents but are not happy to get involved in the care of their partner's parents. Having to consider the needs of our parents and our partner at the same time is often a difficult balance to maintain but it can be brought into greater focus when we retire. Emotions can run high because the feelings we have for our parents run very deep, are rooted in childhood and giving re-assurance to both parent and partners can be stressful. This is particularly at a time when the newly retired partner may require reassurance themselves of their value and worth.

PAUSE FOR THOUGHT

– *Have you and your partner yet embarked on your Expectations Exchange conversation with your own parents?*

– *Are both sets of parents aware of your plans for retirement?*

– *Do they understand the life positives and life challenges you see in your retirement?*

– *Have you discussed the changes that retirement might bring to your relationship with both sets of parents?*

– *What expectations do your parents have of you now that you are retired?*

Relationship changes with ourselves

When we retire other people may think we have lots of time to help out, and we can soon find that our new free time is no longer our own. These may be family members, friends, neighbours, interest groups and voluntary organisations with which we are involved. Unless we have planned ahead and know how much of our time we want to spend in this way, we may find we take on too much for others, and leave no time to take care of ourselves and our dreams. It is as important to honour our own commitment to ourselves in retirement as it is to others.

We started this chapter by talking about the forty hours we now have in retirement to ourselves. For those of us who live alone this might not always be such a welcome prospect. Although our time is literally now our own we would not want it to lie heavily on our hands. Without the additional stimulation of a partner with their own expectations of, and companionship in, retirement we may need to work a little harder to motivate ourselves to replace the easy company of our work colleagues.

However, being alone does not necessarily mean that we are lonely as many of us find enjoyment and solace when sharing our own company. If we take the Present Positive perspective we will now have more time to watch the sunrise, spend time in the garden, prepare our favourite meal, and treat ourselves in our own special way.

Those who live alone by choice have the advantage of not having to make adjustments on retirement for a changing relationship pattern. They still do have to make decisions about where to live, how to create the retirement they want, and make lifestyle options when they are no longer able to be so self-sufficient. The key to a successful retirement for those of us without grown children, grandchildren or other close family members is friendship. It is important not to remain socially isolated and ensure that we have places to go where we are expected, and it is noticed when we do not turn up. If our friendships have been focused at our work then before retirement is the time to find new activities and build new friendships.

....

PAUSE FOR THOUGHT
  - *I would like retirement to be a time in my life when...*
  - *I would like retirement to be a time in my life when I leave behind...*
  - *I would like retirement to be a time in my life when I take forward with me...*

....

Suddenly Alone
For those who shared most of their lives with a partner, widowhood, widowerhood or divorce means a considerable adjustment. Retirement can complicate matters as the benefits we gained from

work, already outlined in previous chapters, are no longer available and the plans we had for a shared retirement are no longer possible. Preparing for such eventualities should play a major part in retirement planning and any discussions between partners that take place about future plans should consider the possibility that one may be left alone without the other.

There is a particular concern currently when men are left alone. Advice given in the report *Isolation: the emerging crisis for older men* by Independent Age is that men approaching later life need to make particular efforts to retain and build their own social network independently among friends, families and interest groups. They may have relied on their partner for most of their life to keep the social contacts going and these can quickly dissipate if continuity is not maintained when the situation changes.

A quote from a contributor to the Report

> *'Isolation is being by yourself.*
> *Loneliness is not liking it.'*

A quote from Mother Teresa

> *'Loneliness and the feeling of being unwanted*
> *is the most terrible poverty.'*

The aim of this book is to encourage you to find your own route to a fun-filled and fear-free retirement. The next chapter explores the complicated issues of enjoyment and happiness.

6

ENJOYMENT AND HAPPINESS

How Can I Find Enjoyment and Happiness In What I Have?

'Happiness is not a thing that can be defined by mathematical formulas. Happiness is no apple that you can peel and eat. If you observe a really happy man you will find him building a boat, writing a symphony, educating his son, growing double dahlias in his garden, or looking for dinosaur eggs in the Gobi desert.'

Wolfe, W. Beran. *How to be Happy Though Human*

There is some discussion about whether there is a difference between pleasure, enjoyment and happiness. Mihaly Csikszentmihalyi spent decades researching the positive aspects of the human experience all over the world. He was searching for the answer to the age old question – when do people feel most happy? And how can we live our lives so that happiness plays a larger part? His view is that pleasure meets an immediate need, but only sustains us for a little time, whereas enjoyment can lead to growth and happiness. In his book *Flow: The Psychology of Happiness: The Classic Work on How to Achieve Happiness,* he writes that contrary to what most of us may believe, happiness does not simply happen to us. It is something we make happen and results from doing our best. The experience of happiness in action is enjoyment, which is the feeling of being fully alive. His theory is that we are at our happiest when we are in a state of 'flow'. We are in a state of 'flow' when we are fully concentrating on or absorbed in a task that we are undertaking. During this state we are carried away by what we are doing, unaware of the time, where we are, and forgetting even our basic needs such as sleep, food and drink. It can be any activity such as work, gardening, a sport, writing, or playing with the children. He calls this 'moving within the current' of an activity allowing it to carry us along, doing it for its own sake, for the feeling it gives us inside, and not for any external reward. We are using our skills to the utmost so that each thought, movement and action flows from the previous one and our whole being is involved. He has called this the challenge-skill balance in which the skill level and the challenge level is high, matched with each other, so that we gain a sense of achievement and having done our best.

Mihaly Csikszentmihalyi believes that it comes more naturally for some than others but, like Beran Wolfe, he believes that everyone can learn how to get into flow and enjoyment in all facets of life. It includes physical and intellectual activities, connecting with others in our work, in solitude and even in times of adversity. The task can be one we already know how to do; something that is completely new to us; or something taxing, problematic; or even tragic. In his view, therefore, enjoyment does not have to be pleasant. It often comes from stretching ourselves, learning new skills, or improving existing ones.

He gives the example of the mountain climber who may be close to freezing, utterly exhausted, and in danger of falling into a bottomless crevasse, yet he would not want to be anywhere else. 'For him or her, sipping a pina colada under a palm tree at the end of a turquoise ocean is idyllic, but it just does not compare to the exhilaration they feel on a windswept ridge.'

PAUSE FOR THOUGHT

- *Can you distinguish between pleasure, enjoyment and happiness in your own life?*

Both Beran Wolfe and Mihaly Csikszentmihalyi both agree that happiness has to be sought rather just pursued, and both agree that it can be learned. Csikszentmihalyi presents the learning as an adventure that requires some intellectual effort, a commitment to reflect and think hard about our own experiences. He recommends that we control the way in which we represent our experiences and interpret the information in our mind. We can learn to enjoy the immediate and transform random events into our own 'flow'.

Although Beran Wolfe discounts the existence of a mathematical formula to define happiness, seventy years later Martin Seligman does provide us with a formula in *Authentic Happiness*. This is an excellent resource with many exercises to help us establish our happiness level. It is based on the research of Sonja Lyubomirsky, set out in her article, *Pursuing Happiness: The Architecture of Sustainable Change*.

The Seligman Happiness Formula is:

H = S (50%) + C (10%) + V (40%)

H is our *enduring level of happiness*

S is our *set range or genetic happiness (50%)*

C is the *circumstances of our life (10%)*

V represents *factors under our voluntary control (40%)*

Sonja Lyubomirsky suggests that our set range of happiness or genetic happiness accounts for only about 50% of our overall happiness; life circumstances for only 10%; and therefore 40% is left under our voluntary control and open for us to change. This offers us all an optimistic view that we can increase H (our enduring level of happiness). The challenge posed is to raise our enduring level of happiness rather than just increasing the number of pleasures or temporary moments of happiness we feel through quick happiness fixes, such as treats, self-rewards and possibly artificial substances.

Our overall happiness is only partly determined by S (our set range or genetic happiness) (50%). Mihaly Csikszentmihalyi would say that we cannot choose our parents, there is not much we can do about our looks, our temperament, personality or our constitution. We cannot decide our date of birth, how tall we grow, our gender or ethnicity. These are genetically determined and are assumed to be fixed and cannot be influenced or controlled.

Our C (life circumstances) (10%) are a relatively stable part of our lives. We cannot choose when and where we were born. This will affect the historical period in which we live and whether we will be affected by war, economic depression or our cultural heritage. Where we are born will affect whether we are exposed to earthquakes, floods or famine. Our own personal history and life situation such as our childhood, job security, marital status, income and health form part of our life circumstances and can have a positive or negative effect on our happiness. Sonja Lyubomirsky suggests that these variables can offer some potential for increasing our happiness levels where we do have some control over our current life situation. We can spend money moving to a new area, we can increase our income, and spend time on our appearance, but these happiness boosts are short-lived and do not produce sustainable change to our happiness level. This is useful information when we are considering making changes when embarking on our retirement.

Our V (voluntary or intentional activity) (40%) has the greatest potential to influence H (enduring level of happiness), as it includes a wide variety of activities that we do every day. They are voluntary and intentional because we can choose to do them, or not do them, and they therefore require some additional conscious effort on our part. Mihaly Csikszentmihalyi says 'Circumstances happen to people and activities are ways that people act on their circumstances'. Voluntary and intentional activities can be behavioural or cognitive. An example of behavioural activity is choosing to do regular exercise, or not. An example of cognitive activity is choosing to re-frame a situation in a more positive light which is encouraged through Positive Psychology and practices such as Cognitive Behavioural Therapy, or not. In Chapter 3, Past Positives were identified as being more inclined to 'count their blessings' and see life as 'half full rather than half empty'. In Chapter 7, the role of Abraham Maslow's self-actualisation identifies the importance of striving for personal goals and fulfilment and devoting effort to causes that have meaning for us. Mihaly Csikszentmihalyi's research indicates that wellbeing increases when we are working towards goals that we have chosen for ourselves, so we are then able to take ownership and control of the subsequent action. This is in contrast to the goals that others may have set for us during our working life and may not 'fit' our own self-concept. Consequently over time we are able to modify our goals to fit our own individual challenge-skill balance.

PAUSE FOR THOUGHT

- *Was there a time in your life when you felt happier than others?*
- *When did you feel at your happiest?*
- *Do you know why?*

Research undertaken by both Sonja Lyubomirsky and Mihaly Csikszentmihalyi highlight the role that effort, making activities habit forming, and appreciation plays in our satisfaction when tackling voluntary and intentional activities. The role of effort can be broken down into the effort of starting an intentional activity and the effort of sustaining it. Some of us are better self-starters than others. However, once we have appreciated the need for investment in our happiness level we may find it easier to sustain even a tedious activity if it fits with our self-concept and values, and we are able to find some meaning and purpose in undertaking it.

It is therefore very re-assuring to know that, even in the later stages of our lives, and particularly in retirement, we can still influence our happiness. Retirement is a time to leave behind any factors that affected thoughts of unhappiness in the past and apply time and effort to intentional activities that positively contribute to our enduring level of happiness.

Curiously, work can often be easier to enjoy than our free time. As mentioned in Chapter 1 it has built in goals, external feedback, a familiar framework within which to operate, and challenges that enable us to become involved, concentrate and lose ourself in our work.

However, hobbies often too require skill, habits that set self-determined goals and limits, personal interest, and an inner discipline that helps turn leisure into 're-creation'. Mihaly Csikszentmihalyi points out that the leisure industry has increasingly been designed to help fill our free time with enjoyable experiences but with passive consumption. He suggests that we are encouraged to buy music to listen to rather than make music ourselves; visit galleries to see the art that others have created rather than make our own art; and watch actors perform 'mock-meaningful' action rather than participate in such action ourselves.

There is a danger that we can be encouraged to spend our retirement years in passive consumption through too much rest and relaxation rather than continuing to participate and involve ourselves in the world around us.

Lisa Steakly writes more simply in *Dream It. List It. Do It! How to Live a Bigger and Bolder Life*. The book starts with some difficult questions that are discussed in the next chapter. However, it ends with hundreds of examples of what makes us happy (besides money). Some of these are:

- having your smile returned by a stranger
- kicking a pile of autumn leaves
- completing a particularly difficult crossword puzzle
- hearing from a long lost friend
- the sudden appearance of a rainbow
- dancing on your own to your favourite music turned up loudly
- finding the perfect present for someone

- taking a fair ride
- an unexpected act of kindness freely given
- coming across a long forgotten favourite book

....

PAUSE FOR THOUGHT

Write the words enjoyment and happiness in the centre of a
large sheet of paper and draw a circle around it. Think about
all the things that you associate with enjoyment and
happiness and write them down. Using different colours
draw lines away from the circle for each of these things and
write a headline word along each line. Draw a branching line
from each of the main lines to show what else you associate
with each of these main ideas

When you have filled in as much as you can, look at the
whole map and ask yourself how you are doing in relation to
each of these areas from 0 – 10 (with 0 being the lowest level
of happiness and 10 being the highest level of happiness)
- *Are you happier in some areas of your life than others?*
- *Which are those areas? Why do you think that might be?*
- *What do you think it will take to increase your enjoyment
  and your enduring level of happiness in those areas?*

....

Philip Zimbardo in *Time Paradox* quotes Sonja Lyubomirsky and gives examples of how happy people tend to spend their time differently from those who are less happy. Each of the chapters in this book provides us with clues to our own happiness formula. He states that happy people:

- **Help and co-operate with others at work** (Chapter 1 How can I Replace the benefits I get from working?)
- **Create their own vision of happiness by setting their own life goals** (Chapter 2 What can I Expect during my transition from work to retirement?)
- **Recognise life's little pleasures and enjoy them in the moment** (Chapter 3 How will I spend my Time?)
- **Cope well with life's challenges** (Chapter 4 Who will I become when I am retired?)
- **Make time for family, friends, and other social relationships** (Chapter 5 How will my Relationships change?)
- **Keep an open mind** (Chapter 6 How will I find Enjoyment and Happiness in what I have?)
- **Stay optimistic about the future** (Chapter 7 Will I find Meaning and Purpose in my retirement?)
- **Are grateful for what they have** (Chapter 8 Will I have Enough money to do what I want to do?)
- **Mix with happy people** (Chapter 5 How will my Relationships change? and Chapter 9 Should I move somewhere New?)

○ **Take regular exercise** (Chapter 10 How should I Take care of myself?)

If happy people seek out happy people then this is the gang to which we would want to belong. From what has been said so far in this chapter it seems clear that the difference between happy retirees and unhappy retirees has less to do with age, education, income level, than it has with our willingness to be happy. Once again Beran Wolfe sums this up:

'(Unhappy people) suffer from an acute stricture of their mental horizon. They are unaware of the breathless drama that moves on the stage of the world all about them. They sit in the wings, twiddling their thumbs, while the sublime tragedy of all time stalks the boards.'

It is not difficult for us to seek out happy people as we have probably been able to recognise them throughout our life. William James in 1884 found that the state of mind, whether positive or negative is mirrored in a matching bodily expression or body behaviour. He says happy people smile more and laugh a lot.

However, there is a lot of disagreement about whether we learn to smile or whether we are born with this ability. The traditional view was that babies learned to smile at about five to seven weeks of age, and any smile before this was regarded as wind. However, with the development of modern technology babies can be seen smiling in the womb at twenty-eight weeks. Lesley Lye in *Laugh Your Way To Happiness: Use the Science of Laughter for Total Well-being* believes that smiling can be adopted as a habit, one of those intentional and voluntary activities. She recognises that there are lots of different types of smiling and they all have a positive effect.

When we make facial changes associated with smiling it stimulates the brain activities associated with happiness. So she believes that putting a smile on our face and keeping it there can affect our whole life, changing the way we feel, and the way other people perceive us and interact with us. The act of smiling is simple but can reap significant rewards in return for little effort. If someone smiles at us the chances are we will smile back. Similarly, if we smile at someone else then they are likely to smile back.

There are many muscles involved in the process of smiling and laughing. It has been estimated that we use around fifty facial muscles to make up to fifty different facial expressions. We can lose the use of these muscles through lack of practice. By smiling and laughing these muscles get a good workout and with repetition they get stronger, and this leads to us looking younger. To get into the habit of smiling takes practice and constant repetition. We can put visual clues around our home reminding us to smile. Lesley Lye recommends that we draw a smiley face on stickers and stick them around the house. In her view within a few days we will feel noticeably happier, but it will take between four and six weeks to develop this into a new voluntary and intentional activity.

PAUSE FOR THOUGHT

– *How often do you catch yourself smiling in a day?*

The same applies to laughter. 'Laughter for no reason' is the core philosophy of Laughter Yoga. Dr Mada Kataria, the Laughing Guru and the founder of Laughter Clubs, sets out his five secrets of laughter in his book *The Inner Spirit of Laughter: Five Secrets from the Laughing Guru:*

- ○ We can train our body and mind to laugh at will
- ○ Laughter is the natural outcome of our playful inner child
- ○ We do not need a sense of humour to laugh
- ○ We can laugh even if we are not in a good mood
- ○ We can laugh even if we are not happy

In his Laughter Clubs a form of group exercise is to laugh at absolutely nothing. This does not mean that there is no reason to laugh. 'The very idea of laughing in a group at nothing is so absurd that it makes us laugh, and we use the infectious and contagious nature of laughter as a reason for simulated laughter'. After they have laughed people tend to keep a smile on their face, and this may be a visual clue to its lasting positive effect on the mood.

....

PAUSE FOR THOUGHT

- *How often do you catch yourself laughing in a day?*
- *Do you go out of your way to find opportunities to laugh or do you expect laughter to come to you?*

....

A final recommendation to improve our enduring level of happiness is made by Helen F McKay, in *Links to your Happiness*. It is to start our own Happy Book and write down at the end of each day the things that have made us happy. 'Acknowledging those things that made us happy is indeed a means to finding the treasures, the joys we store in our memories, every day of our lives'. Over time we can read back through the book and if we are having a 'blue' day then this will help us to tap into many happy memories and lift our mood.

In Chapter 1 we acknowledged that the definition, shape and expectations of retirement are changing significantly. In the past, retirement required us to question very little other than whether we have enough money to support ourselves and our family. It was seen as the opportunity for rest and relaxation. Today we have higher expectations and hope to generate greater satisfaction from the meaning and purpose we can find in our retirement years explained in the next chapter.

7

MEANING AND PURPOSE

Will I Find Meaning and Purpose in my Retirement?

'Creating a happy retirement depends on finding or choosing a life that gives you a new reason to get up in the morning. The challenge is to uncover your passion and choose activities and priorities that make you feel you matter.'

Nancy K Schlossberg *Revitalizing Retirement: Reshaping Your Identity*

There are many retirees who do not look for a purpose, living each day as it comes and choosing routines for the pure enjoyment they offer. Doing nothing in particular may suit us as we feel we have been denied the time and opportunity for rest and relaxation during our working life and while bringing up our families. However, others miss the deadlines and sense of achievement that work brought and when that meaning and purpose is no longer there we recognise that something is missing in our lives. It is time to search for some new meaning, new direction, a new personal mission and create our own personal dream scheme. Four writers provide their ideas to help us search for our own meaning and purpose.

Dr Richard P Johnson in *What Color Is Your Retirement?* claims that the 'new retirement paradigm' goes beyond the pursuit of the pleasure principle of just rest and relaxation in retirement. He asks, 'Where will I find meaning in my life once I no longer work?' since we have probably chosen the kind of work that 'fits' us or we have been able to shape our work to 'fit' us. In doing so we may have found meaning. He argues that for life to be authentic it has to be a journey of meaning.

Meaning however should not be confused with purpose. Meaning is what we feel when we feel useful, a connection with others and a sense that we are doing something necessary and worthwhile. Meaning provides us with a sense that our lives are 'on target'. Meaning gives us the emotional sensation that we are 'in sync' with ourselves and we are balanced and authentic. Lack of life meaning is far more commonly expressed in retirees by a sense of frustration, worthlessness, and internal angst. Meaning comes from recognising that our personality, talents, strengths and values, are being expressed in our daily life.

However, it is more difficult to experience any of this if we do not have a purpose. The purpose is the goal, the objective, the end game, the direction in which we are heading. In our retirement we are entitled to describe our goal as a 'dream with a deadline'.

Viktor E Frankl in *Man's Search for Meaning* argues that the meaning of life differs from man to man, from day to day and from hour to hour. What matters, therefore, is not the meaning of life in general but rather the specific meaning of a person's life at a given moment. His advice is not to aim at success, as the more you aim at it, and make it a target, the more you are going to miss it. 'For satisfaction, like happiness, cannot be pursued... Everyone has his own specific vocation or mission in life to carry out a concrete assignment which demands fulfilment. He cannot be replaced, nor can his life be repeated. Therefore everyone's task is as unique as is his specific opportunity to implement it.'

These writers would contend that we need meaning in order to thrive fully as much as we need the physical elements of air, water and food.

Abraham Maslow over seventy years ago wanted to understand what motivates people to achieve certain needs. He devised his *Hierarchy of Needs* written up in his article *A Theory of Human Motivation* consisting of five motivational needs, biological and physiological, safety needs, love and belonging needs, esteem needs and self-actualisation. Some needs are more basic and therefore more powerful than others. Our basic needs are physiological and survival needs: food, water, sleep, sex etc. At this level our motivation is to seek to obtain the basic necessities of life. Once these needs have been satisfied, we seek safety and security through order and law. Once we feel safe, we are free to pursue love and a sense of belonging and seek affiliation with a group. Our next goal is to seek esteem and self-esteem through recognition and achievement. It is when we meet these goals that we can more fully focus on growth needs that lead to self-actualisation.

Self-actualisation is the need to realise personal potential, self-fulfilment, personal growth, to be fully alive and find meaning in life. As each person is unique the motivation for self-actualisation leads people in different directions. It is an ongoing process of fully developing our personal potential.

While Maslow's theory is generally described as a fairly rigid hierarchy, he noted that the order in which these needs are fulfilled does not always follow this hierarchical progression. For some individuals, the need for self-esteem is more important than the need for love. For others, the need for creative fulfilment may supersede even the most basic needs. 'The specific form that these needs will take, will of course vary greatly from person to person. In one individual it may take the form of the desire to be an ideal mother, in another it may be expressed athletically, and in still another it may be expressed in painting pictures or in inventions.' In his view when we live lives that are different from our true personality, strengths, talents and values, we are less likely to be happy than those whose goals and lives match. In Chapter 6, Csikszentmihalyi describes this process as being in a state of 'flow' to achieve enjoyment and happiness. For example, someone who has an inherent potential to be a great artist or teacher may never realise his/her talents if their energy is focused elsewhere. It was Maslow's belief that self-actualisation can be reached by any particular individual, no matter who they are and irrespective of their personal and economic circumstances. Retirement gives us the opportunity to recapture our inherent potential in a way that the type of work we have undertaken over the years and the time we have had available in the past may not have allowed us to do.

In recent years it became known through the work of Mark E Koltko-Rivera that before Abraham Maslow died he identified a sixth tier of need and human motivation. He referred to this level as self-transcendence. He felt there was a danger that self-actualisation could be perceived as egocentric and selfish behaviour. Ego or self-transcendence is reached when a person develops a deeper sense of purpose, not only focussed on their own needs, but by 'finding meaning in life by connecting their life's journey and happiness to the condition of others, not only those directly around them, but from others all over the world, regardless of race, sex, country or religion.' His view is that they are guided from within, and rely on their inner voices to develop values and rules for living.

Finally, **Lia Steakley** in *Dream It. List It. – How to Live a Bigger and Bolder Life* is a much lighter read although the questions posed at the start of the book are no less demanding. What is it that you would like to do but haven't taken the time or had the motivation to do? and What did you say when you were at school and were asked 'What do you want to do when you grow up?' Did you do it? If not why not?

PAUSE FOR THOUGHT

Take a sheet of paper and draw equal vertical lines for each decade you have lived.

Take yourself back to each decade one by one when there were no limits to your imagined future or the many things you could be and do. For each decade ask yourself

- *What image did you hold of your grown-up self?*
  What image do you hold now?
- *What captured your curiosity? What captures it now?*
- *What excited you? What excites you now?*
- *What made you angry? What makes you angry now?*
- *What moved your heart? What moves it now?*
- *What did you do for fun and enjoyment?*
  What do you do now?
- *Who were the people you most admired and why?*
  Who do you admire now?
- *What causes or problems of the world stirred you?*
  What stirs you now?

Lia Steakley reminds us that somewhere along the line the focus of our dreams have changed 'from what is imaginable to what is attainable; from what is fun to what is practical; from what is risky to what is responsible.' We forget how to dream. If we are in need of inspiration this book provides guidance on how to compile our own Dream Scheme with thousands of ideas, suggestions, practical tips and examples. Many of them will resonate with the ideas we have considered throughout this book.

- ◌ Practise networking amongst new people before we retire so that we start building our new network ready for retirement before we need it (Chapter 1)
- ◌ Make the changes we want in our retirement during the transition from work to retirement rather than allowing the changes to happen to us (Chapter 2)
- ◌ Enjoy the present and take time to pause, rather than continuing to operate in rewind, play and fast-forward (Chapter 3)
- ◌ Continue to reinvent oneself as we create our new identity in retirement (Chapter 4)
- ◌ Keep making new friends as existing relationships change (Chapter 5)
- ◌ Practise being happy as the more we practise the more we experience it (Chapter 6)
- ◌ Continue learning new things (Chapter 7)
- ◌ Sort out the finances (Chapter 8)
- ◌ Be more adventurous and Get out more (Chapter 9)
- ◌ Stay healthy (Chapter 10)

The rules given for creating and conquering our Dream Scheme are:

- ○ Include a mixture of serious and fun dreams as well as vague dreams that can be allowed to simmer away in our mind
- ○ Tell others about our dreams so that they can encourage us
- ○ Treat each dream as a project with its own sense of beginning
- ○ Break each dream down into little goals that are achievable with lots of rewards along the way
- ○ Focus on the start and not the finish
- ○ Record progress from time to time
- ○ Review, revise and remove any dreams that start to become emotionally draining

PAUSE FOR THOUGHT

- *Am I doing what I really want to do with my retirement?*
- *If not, what steps do I need to take to change the situation?*

Having clarified what we want to do in our retirement the next chapter 'Will I have enough money?' attempts to clarify our true financial situation in retirement. This will help us create financial goals that will ensure we have sufficient financial resources that can be channelled to the areas of our life that are important to us. If we have insufficient resources to meet our retirement expectations then we may have to modify either our resources or our expectations of what is enough.

In Chapter 3 we stated that how we spend our time is often an indication of what we think is important. Similarly, how we spend our money is often an indication of what we think is important. What we think is important in the way we live and work is based on our values. They determine our priorities and are probably the measures we use deep down to tell if our life is turning out the way we would want it. When the things that we do and the way we behave match our values then life feels as though it is working out well and we are satisfied. However, when what we are doing does not align with our personal values we often feel that life is not going so well.

As we leave our work behind us and any values associated with that work, retirement is a good time to review our own personal values.

The next exercise provides a starting point for this review. It can be discussed as individuals or with those with whom we are expecting to share our retirement so that we can review our shared values. The outcomes of this discussion will be useful in the next chapter to determine whether we need to make any changes to our financial life if it is to serve our values and meet our financial goals.

....

PAUSE FOR THOUGHT

Identify the times in your career and personal life when you
were happiest
- *What were you doing?*
- *Were you with other people? Who were they?*
- *What other factors contributed to your happiness?*

Identify the times when you felt most satisfied and fulfilled
- *What were you doing?*
- *How and why did the experience give your life satisfaction
  and fulfilment?*
- *What other factors contributed to your sense of
  satisfaction?*

Identify the times when you were most proud
- *What were you proud of?*
- *Were other people as proud as you?*
- *What other factors contributed to your sense of pride?*

....

Below are some examples of common personal values that might
be helpful for the next exercise. There may be others.

Adventure	Ambition	Challenge
Community	Expertise	Fairness

Family	Freedom	Fun
Happiness	Health	Independence
Intellectual status	Learning	Legacy
Love	Loyalty	Making a difference
Patriotism	Peace	Prestige
Power	Security	Success
Trust	Truth	

PAUSE FOR THOUGHT

Draw a circle on a separate piece of paper as below and divide into ten segments. If you are doing this individually then write your core values for life in the ten circle segments. If you have a partner take turns, writing two values each. Then talk about them together

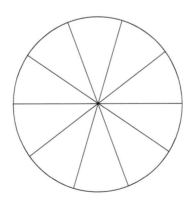

- *Why do you hold these values?*
- *Are there values that you and your partner share?*
- *Are their values that you and your partner do not share?*
- *What did you learn about your values?*
- *Were there any surprises?*

8

ENOUGH

Will I Have Enough Money?

FACTS

○ The median net income after housing costs for pensioners was £282 per week (£404 for pensioner couples and £238 for single pensioners) in last reported year (2012/13)
○ Average weekly spending for households headed by someone aged between sixty-five and seventy-four is £453
○ Average weekly spending for one person households mainly dependent on state pension is £168

Later Life in the United Kingdom– Age UK – May 2015

'Now is no time to think of what you do not have. Think of what you can do with that there is.'

Ernest Hemingway

In terms of retirement planning the area of finances is probably the one that causes us most concern, is the most discussed, and has the greatest impact on our well-being. There appears to be some justification for this as the *Later Life in the United Kingdom* survey by Age UK in 2015 states that 33% of pensioners have less than £1,500 in savings and 18% of single pensioners and 5% of couple pensioners have no source of income other than the state pension and benefits.

Like everything else the financial dimension of retirement preparation is also changing. In the past we have relied on our employers and the State to make provision for our retirement. However, now retirement funding sits squarely on the shoulders of the individual and during 2015-2017 legislation requires all UK employers to enrol their employees into a pension scheme, with both being required to contribute. A percentage of retirees are delaying retirement or returning to work and taking up second, third, bridge or retirement careers. Some retirees are starting up businesses or continuing careers by taking on a consultancy role. This process is called 'pre-tirement' rather than retirement. Others are taking the opportunity to combine long held personal passions and dreams with financial needs by creating personally fulfilling pre-tirement work.

For most of us, unless we win the Lottery it is too late to add substantial gains to our retirement wealth. It is therefore comforting to know that retirees who judge themselves as financially comfortable generally recognise the difference between a high quality of life and a high standard of living. Those who consider that they have a high quality of life equate this with high levels of self-esteem and life satisfaction, are more socially involved and participate in more volunteer activities.

None of these necessarily require lots of money. Since childhood we have been told that money does not bring happiness, or that merely having enough money is no guarantee of a life worth living or of retirement satisfaction. However, we cannot deny that it does play a central role in overall satisfaction in retirement. Therefore, if we are not in a position to accumulate new wealth then we may need to shift our focus to making the best possible use of the rest of our assets – our time, our strengths and our talents. This will include experiencing all the special moments and pleasure that do not necessarily require money. Much of our satisfaction during retirement may have to come from how well we understand our own personal relationship with, and attitude to, money, and how we can reconcile our actual retirement budget with our personal meaning of what is enough.

In her very helpful book *Be Your Own Financial Adviser* Jonquil Lowe recognises that one of the frustrations of financial planning is that, however carefully we may plan, we are still facing the unknown, in terms of the economy and what may happen in our personal lives. Inflation rates and rates of return on our investments cannot be predicted in the long term and financial past performance is no guarantee of future performance.

In addition, we do not know how long we will live, and so it is difficult to know how many years we should be planning for. In addition, until we have decided on the type of lifestyle we would like to have in our retirement it is difficult to predict the level of income we require. In the words of John Lennon in 'Beautiful Boy (Darling Boy)', 'Life is just what happens to you while you're busy making other plans'. We may need money for unforeseen events such as health care in later life, supplementing our income, legal fees, relationship breakdown, helping adult children out of financial difficulties.

However, many of us did not learn financial management skills from our parents and may not have felt the need to learn the basics of financial planning while we were still earning. Some of us have not been disciplined in our financial management. In the past, in many families, financial issues were not discussed, and children were actively discouraged from asking their parents about the family income, what it cost to pay the bills, or how much they had saved for retirement.

Although at retirement we possibly enjoy our highest net worth, the realisation that when we leave work we leave our regular income behind, possibly forever, never to be replenished, is a frightening prospect. However, now is the time to get to grips with that fear, honestly face the question of 'What is enough?' and understand when enough is enough. The financial equation is simple:

If more money leaves our bank account than goes in then we are likely to have an uncomfortable retirement.

Below is a nine step plan to help us take control of our retirement finances.

Step 1 – What do I want to do in my retirement?

There is no easy way to predict the amount of income we will need or want when we come to retire. Financial advisers suggest that we should aim for two-thirds or perhaps half of our current earnings. We may spend less on tax, pension contributions, travelling to work and work related expenditure, but we may spend more on moving home, travelling the world, leisure related expenditure, health problems and heating. There are countless books on retirement planning but the basis of this book is to determine our values and priorities so that we can allocate our financial resources to the areas of our life that are important to us. Each of our financial goals should be based on our values. The purpose of this chapter is to tease out the answers to the following questions:

PAUSE FOR THOUGHT

You may wish to complete this with your partner or separately and then discuss it together
- *What do I need in my daily life of retirement?*
- *What is necessary and what is nice to have?*
- *What does living well mean to me?*
- *How much do I need to live well?*
- *What money do I need to follow my passions?*
- *What does 'enough' mean to me?*

Step 2 – How much do I spend now, and on what?

Possibly for the first time ever we are being asked to make a true and accurate list of what comes in and what goes out of our bank account.

PAUSE FOR THOUGHT
- *What is your income?*
- *What is your expenditure?*
- *What is the difference ?*

Our Income may include earnings, benefits, pensions, maintenance, interest from savings, income from investments, rental etc. Our Expenditure will include mortgage payments, rent, council tax, regular household bills, phone, internet, TV, insurances, home maintenance, household goods, food, alcohol, clothing, footwear, motoring costs, holidays, leisure activities, presents, donations, savings, investments, pension contributions, loan repayment, etc. This will give us a true and accurate picture of our current spending.

Step 3 – How much income will I have to meet my future needs?

We can establish our current financial situation by calculating our expenditure from our income and hopefully arriving at a positive sum. It is now time to establish our real worth. We need to complete a Balance Sheet to include our Assets such as investments, savings, property, antiques, paintings, pensions. On the Liabilities side to include overdraft, bills in arrears, credit and store debit cards, personal loans, mortgage, etc.

This will help us to see in what proportion of types of assets our retirement resources are invested. Although we may see our retirement plan as a household plan, pension schemes are personal to each member of the household. For example, this means that as a couple we should be considering what would happen if the relationship were to break down and our pension rights split as an asset, or one should regrettably die. If we are not married neither partner has a claim on each other's pension. This is the time to:

- Search for all your financial documents and put them together – there may be some Premium Bonds, ISAs, or shares to chase up for up-to-date evaluation.
- List all your employers and check to see if you have any pension rights (www.gov.uk/find-lost-pension)
- Get an up-to-date estimate of your state pension (www.gov.uk/state-pension-statement)
- Get an up-to-date estimate of your occupational pension
- If you are divorced, or going to be, check on any pension rights and retirement assets to which you are entitled from your ex's career history. This may be more valuable than retaining the family home.

Once we have estimated our pension pot, there are a number of decisions to be made about the different ways we can take money from that pot. The number of choices available have been increased since April 2015. Information can be found at Pension Wise (www.pensionwise.gov.uk)

Step 4 – How much income do I need?

Now is the time to decide how much income we need to do all the things we promised ourselves in Step 1. This is our target income. According to Age UK's *Later Life in the United Kingdom* survey, the average weekly spending for households headed by someone aged between sixty-five and seventy-four is £453; and the average weekly spending for one-person households mainly dependent on state pension is £168.

This includes food and non-alcoholic drinks, alcoholic drinks, tobacco, clothing and footwear, housing, fuel and power, household goods and services, health, transport, communication, recreation and culture, education, restaurants and hotels, and miscellaneous goods and services.

Step 5 – Will I have 'enough'?

Compare the annual projected income in Step 3 with the annual projected expenditure in Step 4 during retirement and work out the difference. Do we have enough or do we need to save more now, earn more now, or retire later? If we cannot defer retirement what steps can we take to earn during retirement, or will we spend less?

PAUSE FOR THOUGHT

Can you take advantage of any of these?

- *Re-organise any debts*
- *Make the most of your home equity by paying off your mortgage, selling your current home and downsizing to finance your retirement, take out a home equity loan to pay for another house for rental income*
- *Move to a less expensive location (Chapter 9)*
- *Rent out one of your bedrooms, possibly to a struggling University student*
- *Learn more about managing your finances by going on a money management or financial planning course, joining an investment club*
- *Pay more attention to your retirement resources*
- *Reduce your financial responsibilities for others*
- *Put an end to impulse spending and make less expensive choices*
- *Find pleasure in cheaper activities*
- *Find work that is both rewarding and offers a salary*
- *Change your relationship with money (Step 6)*
- *Get help from an expert you can trust (Step 7)*
- *Establish more effective budgeting habits and stick to them (Step 8)*
- *Ask yourself if you can afford to leave the legacy you intended (Step 9)*

Step 6 – What will I have to do differently?

Having undertaken the above exercise we may be very pleasantly surprised at just how financially astute we have been. On the other hand, we may be fooling ourselves and living beyond our means even before we have to consider how we will live on a reduced income in retirement. We may have succumbed to 'conspicuous and competitive consumption' and we may be in the habit of buying things for the sake of buying them and keeping up appearances. Retirement is an opportunity to recognise the need to simplify our lives and re-think the role money plays in our lives and our relationship with it.

Our relationship with and confidence in money is largely influenced by the attitudes we have inherited and by the behaviours we observed or acquired throughout our life. Marika and Howard Stone in *Too Young to Retire* state that, '… If we were fortunate to grow up in a family with money then we are likely to be confident about our ability to make and manage money. If our parents were always concerned about money and had to watch every penny then we too may be fearful. Now is the time to unhook ourselves from that past conditioning.'

Our financial confidence is not necessarily related to how much money we have. Someone may have spent all their life accumulating a large retirement pot because they perceive retirement as very expensive and going on forever. They may be fearful because they have seen family and friends struggling and have had to help them out in later years. They have believed from an early age that if you are not working you do not deserve to receive a decent income.

On the other hand someone else has a much smaller pot, always worked for the same company, has a guaranteed pension, had a regular salary coming in, and believes that it is going to be quite adequate for their needs. They have never seen anyone struggle, think of retirement as a much shorter period, and that if they run out of money then the Government will support them. One has enough but is fearful, the other may not have enough but is not fearful at all. Our financial confidence is developed through the thoughts we put in our mind from our perceptions, and our perceptions emerge from our beliefs, attitudes and values towards money.

In Chapter 3, we established that possibly our only true personal asset is time and therefore we must treat retirement as the challenge of finding the best possible use of the time we have left. If we are focussing on the experience of all the special moments and pleasures that do not require money then it may only play a minor role. Following through the ideas in *Time Paradox* by Philip Zimbardo outlined in Chapter 3 there is a link between our relationship with time and our relationship with money.

Pasts are concerned to keep what they have rather than enjoying what they have today or saving for tomorrow. They are unlikely to take risks and concentrate on their needs rather than their wants.

Presents have one of two attitudes towards money. Present Fatalists treat money as though it does not matter as the lessons of the past are irrelevant and investments in the future are unlikely to be successful. Money does not hold the key to the past or to the future and they believe how much or little they have is beyond their control. Present Hedonists enjoy money right now, without thought of the past or expectations of the future, to create fun and excitement. Philip Zimbardo said 'They never expect it to rain so they do not save for a rainy day. When it does, they dry out quickly and revert back to their old ways.' They often pay more than once for everything they buy, once the first time and then again and again in credit card interest payments and late fees.

Futures balance their books more frequently than those lower on the future time perspective scale. They pay their bills on time, save for the future, and keep their eye on their statements and investments. For them money represents future possibilities that they did not have yesterday and do not have today.

Changing our relationship with money may not be as easy as changing our relationship with time. However, we can use our efforts in one area to complement changes in the other. As with our use of time, if we have a balance of past positive, present hedonism and future time perspectives in our relationship with money then we are able to continue to learn from the past, enjoy the present and plan for the future.

Step 7 – Should I engage a Financial Adviser?

The process of finding a good financial adviser is the same as for any service we are accessing. Advisers giving advice about pensions and investments can no longer be paid by commission but now charge fees. Everyone who has a defined-contribution pension scheme is entitled to a free guidance session with Pension Wise (www.pensionwise.gov.uk).

○ Ensure they hold the necessary qualification and indemnity insurance by checking with the Financial Services Authority (www.fsa.gov.uk/register/home.do)

○ Ask your friends and family to make recommendations, but still check with the Financial Services Authority

○ Ask if they provide a free initial session so that you make your own judgement and whether you feel comfortable with them

○ Check that they have clients in a similar financial situation as yourself

○ Ask upon what areas they can provide advice

Step 8 – How will I keep on track?

If we are adopting new and better financial management strategies and habits, it is particularly important to keep these up during retirement, so that we can continue to meet our needs even when other more interesting distractions can get in the way. We will need to keep all our documentation up-to-date and compile a quarterly report for ourselves so that we are continually monitoring our retirement resources. Our investments may earn less interest, interest rates may rise, our personal circumstances may change, we may need to change our Will, and we may make some financial mistakes along the way. If we have engaged a Financial Adviser it is important to keep him or her on their toes.

Step 9 – Leaving a Legacy

The financial services industry would have us believe that leaving a legacy is all about maximising the estate we can leave our children and minimising our inheritance tax. This might be the first time we have thought about leaving behind something when we have gone. However, our legacy does not have to be a financial legacy. As parents, grandparents, teachers, mentors, collectors of art, creators of art, we can teach those who will be there when we are gone.

In Chapter 7 Abraham Maslow referred to our need for ego or self-transcendence which is our need to help others gain their own self-actualisation. This is our capacity to:

- feel pleasure in the pleasures of others
- be concerned about events not directly related to our self-interest
- invest in tomorrow's world although we will not be around to see it

An investment in the future through the leaving of a legacy can help enhance the quality of old age. But so does a stronger emphasis on the pleasures of the moment and a capacity to live in the here and now. In a good growing old we can stop obsessing about time running out and learn to fully inhabit the time we are in, acquiring a sense of Presentness (Chapter 3)

'I had an inheritance from my Father.
It was the moon and sun.
And thus I roam all over the world.
The spending of it's never done'

Ernest Hemingway

I Wish you Enough

I wish you enough sun to keep your outlook bright

I wish you enough rain to appreciate the sun more

I wish you enough happiness to keep your spirit alive

I wish you enough pain to make life's joys seem precious

I wish you enough luck to satisfy your needs

I wish you enough gain to satisfy your wanting

I wish you enough loss to appreciate all that you possess

I wish enough 'Hellos' to get you through the final 'Good-bye'

Anon

One of the most important decisions that we have to make when we retire is where we will live now that we are not fixed to the locality in which we worked. The next chapter will help you to explore and clarify your sense of place, what home means to you, and how you may adapt your current home or create your next home.

9

NEW LOCATION
Should I Move To
Somewhere New?

FACTS

Housing

- Currently 9.3 million households are headed by a person over retirement age. By 2033, this is expected to increase to 13 million
- More than 20% of individuals aged fifty or older in England, have no housing wealth at all
- 67% (1.1 million people) of older people living in poverty are owner occupiers

Loneliness and Isolation

- People with a high degree of loneliness are twice as likely to develop Alzheimer's than people with a low degree of loneliness
- 36% (3.8 million) of over sixty-fives live alone. 70% of these are women 49% of over seventy-fives live alone
- Over 10% (1 million) older people say they are always or often feel lonely
- 37% (4 million) of over sixty-fives consider television as their main form of company
- 12% of over sixty-fives said they never spent time with their family
- 17% have less than weekly contact with family, friends and neighbours
- 11% have less then monthly contact with family, friends and neighbours

Later Life in the United Kingdom – Age UK – May 2015

147

Where and how we live in later life is not only a major concern for each of us, but it should be a major concern for government and housing think-tanks. In our Facts we set out that by 2033 the number of households headed by a person over retirement age is expected to increase to 13 million; an increase of 40% on figures for 2008. The Chartered Institute of Housing (CIH) in its report *New Approaches to Housing for Older People* states, 'Being older can last a long time – policy approaches should look at an age range from 55 to over 100'.

The challenge is to ensure that models of bespoke housing for older people could be developed in the future that enables

- increasing numbers of older people to have better and more attractive housing options that provide more fit for purpose affordable solutions to their housing needs.
- health and care services when needed to be delivered closer to home, providing better outcomes for older people and achieving savings for the public purse, by reducing dependence on acute services.
- older people to have a living environment that promotes personal safety, social engagement and activity, maximising wellbeing and reducing the ill effects of social isolation and the adverse impacts of some long term conditions.

It is also a challenge that 26.1% (2 million households) of the homes occupied by over sixties in England already fail the decent homes standard according to the Age UK *Later Life in the UK* report published in September 2014.

One of the most important decisions that we have to make when we retire is where we will live now that we are not fixed to the locality in which we worked. This chapter will help us clarify what home means to us and our sense of place. It will also explore the many options we have as we search for the situation that best fits our needs, values, lifestyle and income.

....

PAUSE FOR THOUGHT

You may wish to complete this on your own first and then with your partner

– *Home to me is…*
– *What are the favourite spaces in your home?*
– *Where are your fondest memories in your home?*
– *What do you most value about your home and your neighbourhood?*
– *If you knew you were going to stay there for the rest of your life, what changes would you make?*
– *What would you do if your finances no longer allowed you to live in your current home?*

....

At one end of the spectrum for some retirees, there is no decision to make. We will stay where we are, remain in the same house, near our children or other family members or friends and will not change a thing. This can work well as long as both members of the couple agree. However, it is surprising that many people come to retirement not having really thought about and discussed this issue honestly and openly, often having made only fleeting references to the future during retirement conversations over the years.

At the other end of the spectrum retirees can sell up and take off for full time travel, either within their own country or abroad. Between these two options there is a range of possibilities to consider. One of the most costly mistakes people can make in retirement is to move house without giving sufficient thought to the possible consequences, as there are both financial and emotional costs involved in moving somewhere new.

It can be as expensive to move down the road within the same town as it can be to moving to another part of the country. Moving home is within the same category of emotional life-changing events as divorce, dissolving a relationship, losing a partner, being made redundant. We are therefore advised not to move too soon after retirement. Although a new beginning is attractive in these circumstances the decision should be made calmly, carefully and for the right reasons.

....

PAUSE FOR THOUGHT

- *Is it possible that by relocating you are running away from something that will follow you wherever you go?*
- *Are you running towards something without exactly knowing what you will find?*
- *If you are moving as part of a couple, is one of you more enthusiastic about the idea than the other and therefore will the move serve both of your interests?*
- *If your extended family is an important part of your social and emotional life will you miss them by moving away?*
- *Do you value the company of old friends rather than making new friends?*
- *How important is the familiarity of your home and the area in which you live? Will the new home/area compensate sufficiently for their loss?*
- *Have you considered renting your house for a year so that you can come back home if you wish?*
- *What would you do if you can no longer drive?*
- *What would you do if your partner was no longer with you?*

....

One challenge to be acknowledged is that in most new locations we will be starting over again and it is therefore important that we can be sure of establishing new support networks. To fit in, we must make the effort in the beginning to earn the respect of those around us, rather than feeling that we deserve it based on our past.

There are a number of reasons why we tend to move when we retire.

Relocating to a beautiful location and find peace

🙂 It can be near the sea with sandy beaches, surrounded by mountains for walking and skiing, in the middle of forest and woodland that change colour with the seasons. It can be a place where we spent our holidays, which is familiar and full of happy memories.

🙁 Holidays are fun because they take us out of our routine. Once retirement becomes routine it might not have the same attraction. It is important that we spend time there out of the holiday season as it may look differently out of season.

Moving to a warmer climate

🙂 Waking up to blue skies, sunshine and warmth every day in retirement is particularly tempting if the damp and the cold in this country has had an adverse effect on our physical health, wellbeing and mental health.

🙁 Some countries get too hot at certain times of year and we will need to organise some kind of escape. Air conditioning can also adversely affect our health.

Changing country

🙂 There are 196 countries in the world bursting with interesting and exotic cultures, foods, experiences, landscapes, religious practices, languages, art, music, and living conditions. Retirement is a time to experience somewhere different. If there are not many British people living in our area then we too might become interesting and exotic.

☹ Check out the strength of the currency, necessity of learning the language, exchange rate fluctuations, inflation rates, tax systems, the reliability of their banks (!), entitlement to the health services, stability of property prices, safety and security. Some governments do not allow foreigners to buy property, cost of flights home in the long-term. Adopted countries may not feel like home and there may be some life positives we are leaving behind that cannot be replaced. If we move to an area where there are many British expatriates this may not be as interesting and exotic as we imagined. Finally it would be sensible to develop an exit strategy if the experience does not meet our expectations.

Returning to the home of your birth

🙂 Our working life is over and our dream is being fulfilled. At last we feel we are back home where we belong surrounded by family, friends, and familiarity.

☹ Try out the dreams before it becomes a reality and our decision is irreversible. The warm welcome we received when we visited on holiday may not feel so warm when our presence is no longer a novelty. We may miss the family, friends and familiarity of our adopted country.

To be closer to a support structure

☺ This is often the biggest factor of all in determining where many couples will live. *The Later Life survey* (May 2015) revealed that 12% of people over sixty-five never saw their family. Living near our family provides re-assurance for them and for us that we will have physical and emotional support during our retirement. Having contact with the younger generation keeps us up-to-date with the pace of modern life and involved in society. It also gives us a purpose when we know there is something we can contribute to our lives and somewhere we are expected.

☹ Some couples cannot agree between themselves how much contact they want with their family. Children and their partners may also not agree between themselves. Moving closer to family does not always meet expectations. Younger family members may themselves move again, leaving us on our own in the place where we were expecting a support system for the rest of our life.

Moving closer to or with friends

☺ Some retirees decide that the future is better spent in the company of friends rather than family and moving near to or with them becomes a priority in retirement. Some friends move simultaneously to a new area, buy land or property together, or co-own two houses in different climates. If our adult children tend to move around then this might be a more convenient arrangement.

☺ Friends can fall out and if disillusionment sets in on the part of one couple or one of the individuals within a couple then everyone is affected. If one of the couple's circumstances change or one dies, then the dynamics of the relationship can also change. It may be more sensible that we all make new and maybe different friends from each other in our new location rather than just relying on the same friends.

Moving out of the city for a lower cost of living

☹ When we no longer have to live in the city for work then moving somewhere where the cost of living is lower is a great way of bridging a gap in retirement income. Somewhere smaller can often prove friendlier and easier to make new contacts and get involved in local activities. It will probably also be easier to park outside our home.

☺ Leaving the city for a smaller town or the country may mean there are fewer shops, health facilities, attractions and activities, less easy access to motorways, and the public transport is less convenient and more expensive than in the city. It is also more likely that we will find more opportunities to earn an income if we stay in the city.

Moving from the country to the city

🙂 Some retirees decide to move the other way and leave the country for the city, which will give more opportunities for entertainment, better nightlife, access to culture, better transport links, safety and security, possibly closer to family, nearer to medical facilities, no driving, compact living, vibrant surroundings, less isolation, and earned income opportunities.

🙁 If we have spent most of our life in the country it is important to recognise that we might miss the clean air, sound of the birds, our horses and livestock, accessible sunrises and sunsets, trees, slower pace, friendly neighbours, and the countryside. Property prices in the city are likely to be higher and therefore the space we will acquire will be much smaller. Parking may also be a problem if we still need a car to retain independence.

Moving to a bigger house

🙂 When couples retire and both spend more time in the home some retirees feel that this is the time to move to a bigger house rather than downsize. There is more space to have the grandchildren to stay, friends and family to visit, to spread out, and to create a space for both sets of hobbies. As we get older there is a tendency for couples to have separate bedrooms, their own studies, and bathrooms.

☹ There may be an increase in the cost of financing the property, heating, household expenses, as well as more cleaning and more maintenance. Increasingly children and grandchildren are finding it difficult to get on the property ladder and either do not move out of the family home, or move in while sorting out accommodation. Moving to a bigger home might encourage this with the consequent added burden of meeting their living expenses. There might therefore not be the space you envisioned.

Downsizing to a smaller home

☺ When we retire it is highly likely that our children will have already moved out. Therefore retirement is a good opportunity to re-evaluate our lifestyle. Downsizing allows us to get rid of significant home maintenance demands and reap the cost benefit and reduction in household care. If our children have not left home then this might be the time to encourage them to do so.

☹ However, if we are already feeling the loss of status from our disengagement from work, having to downsize might contribute to our diminished feeling of self-worth. As a couple we will be learning to spend more time together, and in a smaller space than we have been used to. This will also require some serious de-cluttering and moving from a family home that probably holds years of happy memories.

Living in two homes and two locations

☺ If we and our partner cannot agree then an ideal solution is to live in two locations. Many people have a home in the UK and a home in the sun giving them the advantages of a warm climate and a change of scene without losing the sense of security and well-being that familiarity can bring, plus all the free health benefits of the National Health Service.

☹ Maintaining two homes is twice the work and twice the cost. Keeping up our networks and friendship groups in both places also means twice the effort.

Moving to a differently designed home

☺ Having evaluated our future lifestyle we may decide to move to a house that has already been adapted for elder living; move and adapt a new house; or adapt our existing house. These features would include low cost heating, little maintenance, outside space with limited maintenance, security systems, good lighting, wiring for new technology, probably one storey, plenty of accessible storage, dining table that expands for two to ten people, en suite bathrooms, wheel chair friendly, easy nonslip bathtubs, skid-proof tiles, gentle graded walkways and parking close by.

☹ It is probably not easy to find a house that is the perfect fit with the perfect fittings in the perfect location. If we decide to make the adjustments ourselves then it will obviously be costly and disruptive in the short term.

Moving to a different style of living

☺ Many people anticipate the danger of isolation and loneliness in later life by moving into shared housing. There are a number of options, including retirement villages, retirement communities, shared apartments, retirement homes, and co-housing community. An innovative example of the latter is the Older Women's Co-Housing development in High Barnet http://www.owch.org.uk. The advantages of living in bespoke accommodation with a group of like-minded, ready-made and age-ready friends on our door step are considerable. While saving cost and effort, it can allow us to perform our necessary day to day tasks with independence, still having time to satisfy our physical, mental and emotional needs.

☹ A great deal of thought is required before signing on the dotted line and giving up our home to take up independent living options in retirement villages, retirement communities or co-housing communities as there may be no way of going back. A new development needs time to fill with people, to build a community and develop its own culture. Living in a half empty community waiting to see if it will fill can be frustrating. It is

NO FEAR RETIREMENT

important to clearly understand the role of freeholders, managing agents, arrangements for guests staying, service charges, subletting arrangements, exit fees, re-sale conditions. The role and strength of the residence association will be important once the developers have moved out and the management companies move in. Regular residents' meetings can flag up issues before they become a major concern. If residents are sharing space then there is always the potential for in-house disputes. For example, if there is a residents' lounge, who controls the remote control? We would want to ensure that we integrate into the life of the community and that we are not controlled by it.

Whether we stay where we are or we decide to move, time in retirement provides us with two ideal opportunities – to re-connect with our sense of home and to de-clutter.

By the time we retire we will be an expert in creating a home, maybe a number of homes. Much time, effort, money and emotion has been invested in our home/s over the years. In *Making a House a Home* Clare Nolan recognises that, 'home is the place where we have brought up our family, that has provided us with a sanctuary in times of difficulty, that has allowed us to be creative, productive and nurturing'.

Over the years as we have moved through our different life phases we may have built up and added to our home, piece of furniture by piece of furniture, and room by room, rather than standing back and look at the style we have created as a whole. In retirement we have the opportunity to revise our own version of our home and make changes that reflect our new life in retirement.

Her advice is not to throw things out unnecessarily and buy things new, but by seeing the familiar differently it can change our outlook and re-invigorate this aspect of our life in retirement.

It can be done by changing the room layout, moving furniture into different rooms, re-painting, re-upholstering, swapping paintings around, changing the lighting. Flowers, different fragrances and changing our accessories can be used to reflect the changing seasons.

There are some questions at the end of the chapter for you to further reflect on your sense of home and build that into your plans.

If we are moving to a smaller house then we will be motivated to de-clutter through necessity and this will undoubtedly form a very large project. If we are staying in our house then there is no longer any excuse for not spending time having a good sort out. We may be motivated by pressure from others around us, the promise of a sense of achievement at the end, and the need to 'let go', 'move through' and 'move on' from our working world. It will be important to ensure that motivation remains with us throughout the process.

There are many books on de-cluttering and just one is referenced here. *Unclutter Your Life in One Week* by Erin Rooney Doland provides a de-cluttering programme that covers all areas of the home in one week.

As Erin Rooney Doland states, 'Sentimental clutter can be the hardest type to conquer'. However, '… it is important to remember the past, but an unclutterer does not live in it…' She has some tips that sound simple but might be more difficult to execute in reality:

○ Take a photo of the object rather than keeping the object itself and complement the photo with notes about the memory. It can also be turned into some form of art work.

○ There is no need to keep every item of a dinner service, for example, it might be possible to keep a plate and either make use of it or display it.

○ Papers as well as pictures can be scanned and turned into digital files.

○ If we are keeping letters from old friends, or penfriends, for example, once these have been scanned we can return them to the originator and have a fun time reminiscing.

○ Scraps of old clothes can be kept and made into a quilt to be used or a collage to be displayed.

◌ Gifts can be passed on to someone else. If it gave us a moment of happiness then we can re-cycle that moment for someone else.

◌ Make the goodbyes to our belongings as speedy as we can.

Having taken the time and care to decide where we want to live and how we want to live our retirement years the final chapter emphasises the importance of taking time and care to prioritise ourselves and our well-being now that we have the additional time to spare.

10

TAKING CARE
How Should I take
Care of Myself?

Previous chapters have encouraged us to think about our future and with whom we want to spend our retirement years. We have considered our own expectations, the expectations that others have of us, how we will spend our time, who we want to be, the impact of retirement on our relationships, our financial position, how we will find meaning and purpose and enjoyment and happiness, and where we want to live out our retirement years.

We are expecting to continue to enjoy those things we are doing today as well as being involved in activities we have never before had time to do. However, following through on the decisions we have made, and the conclusions we have come to as a result of our reflections, will depend on our own sense of well-being and our level of physical, mental, social and spiritual fitness once we have retired.

It is highly likely that the first decade of our retirement will provide us with the greatest opportunity and the most fulfilment. After that it is more likely that health problems will intervene and may limit what we can do.

Even if we do not expect to make too many drastic changes to our lifestyle, and we want to continue doing what we enjoy doing now, it is important that we visualise ourselves a few years on and anticipate any adjustments we may need to make now and act on them. Poor health will disrupt our plans; restrict our freedom; make us dependent on others; and reduce our self-esteem. If we are in a partnership, the health of either partner can make the adjustment to retirement much more difficult for both.

This is a particularly difficult chapter to write as there is a wide variation between individuals as to their actual health status, their fitness, and their own self-perception of their health and well-being in retirement. Many features of our health were determined by our genetic potential at the moment of our conception. The factors in our early life will have had an effect on our health now. In addition, the habits we have acquired during the course of our adult life, such as smoking, drinking, eating an unwise diet, and the level of exercise we have chosen, or been able to undertake, may have had an adverse effect on our health now.

There is no shortage of health information, and advice is already available to us wherever we look The challenge is to turn all that advice into action.

Retirement finally gives us the opportunity to put ourselves at the top of our priority list and to make taking care of ourselves the focus of our day. We can spend some of that new spare time we have each day on activities that will contribute to our own physical, mental, social and spiritual well-being if we choose to do so. It is possible that until now we have taken our good health for granted without appreciating how lucky we have been. On the other hand, it is possible that we have got used to our existing state of well-being and have not realised how much better we might feel, and our body might perform, if we were to make some changes.

Our physical well-being includes our health, fitness, weight and our appearance. This can be affected by the diet we follow, the amount of exercise we take, and the image we choose to present to the outside world.

....

PAUSE FOR THOUGHT (seek professional advice where appropriate)

I would describe my health and well-being as...

I am satisfied with the following aspects of my physical well-being...

but now that I have the time I could make improvements on a daily basis by...

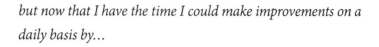

Our mental well-being includes developing a healthy and positive attitude to life, living a life based on our personal values, developing a life-long aptitude for learning and personal growth, and establishing a curiosity and a base of useful knowledge that continually requires updating. We have already taken the opportunity to develop our own happiness formula and measure our number of happy and satisfied days compared with our sad, depressed and unsatisfied days by completing our Happy Book outlined in Chapter 6.

PAUSE FOR THOUGHT

I am satisfied with the following aspects of my mental well-being...

but now I have the time I could make improvements on a daily basis by…

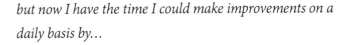

Spiritual well-being includes becoming aware of our life's meaning and purpose, developing our innate gifts, and using our talents in a positive way. Spirituality can mean following a faith or a higher power, but it can also mean that being in touch with our own spirituality implies a greater sense of awareness of ourselves, others and what is going on around us. In Chapter 3 we referred to Mindfulness and being more present in the moment rather than in the past or in the future.

PAUSE FOR THOUGHT
I am satisfied with the following aspects of my spiritual well-being…

but now I have the time I could make improvements on a daily basis by...

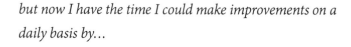

Social well-being includes the careful creation and maintenance of healthy and positive relationships, our contribution and involvement in the community, and our impact on our surroundings or environment. As mentioned in Chapter 5 relationships can have a detrimental or positive effect on our well-being, and retirement is a time to review the quality of our relationships with family, friends, neighbours and acquaintances and decide which we will continue to nurture and grow and which to minimise, avoid or end.

Individuals differ in the amount of time they wish to devote to their local community and to their surroundings and the environment. Retirement does, however, provide the time to re-assess our connectedness, the contribution we can make, and the amount of involvement we can have to improve and protect what we have around us to the best of our ability. Preserving this becomes even more important as we ourselves get older and rely on our own locality to stimulate our interest and provide companionship.

....

PAUSE FOR THOUGHT

I am satisfied with the following aspects of my social well-being...

but now I have the time I could make improvements on a daily basis by...

....

The questions we have asked ourselves will help to review our physical, mental, social and spiritual well-being and establish the areas that could inhibit our retirement plans through ill health if they are neglected. As a result of the review we can develop our personal daily care contract that we can make with ourselves. Below is an example of an A-Z daily plan with links to relevant websites which starts the day by waking up with a positive attitude to the day and ends the day with a touch of zing.

Your A-Z Daily Dose of Care

Attitude (Mental well-being)
Are you waking up with a positive attitude to the day?
Find your care here...
- http://www.helpguide.org/articles/aging-well/staying-healthy-as-you-age.htm

Brain fitness (Mental well-being)
Are you keeping your brain fit and your mind active by learning something new each day?
Find your care here...
- http://www.ageuk.org.uk/health-wellbeing/keeping-your-body-healthy/13-steps-to-better-health

Conversation (Social well-being)
Are you having a conversation with at least one person each day either face to face, telephone or email?
Find your care here...
- http://www.gretchenrubin.com/happiness_project/2009/05/seven-tips-for-making-good-conversation-with-a-stranger/

Diet (Physical well-being)
Does your diet have the right balance of high fibre, fruits, vegetables and whole grains, vitamins, minerals and water to complement the ageing process?

Find your care here...

- http://www.ageuk.org.uk/health-wellbeing/healthy-eating-landing/healthy-eating-overview/eating-well

Exercise (Physical well-being)

Does your daily exercise include activities that are improving your strength, stamina, balance and suppleness?

Find your care here...

Exercises for strength

- http://www.nhs.uk/Livewell/fitness/Pages/strength-exercises-for-older-people.aspx

Exercises for stamina

- http://www.nhs.uk/livewell/loseweight/pages/10000steps challenge.aspx

Exercises for balance

- http://www.nhs.uk/Livewell/fitness/Pages/balance-exercises-for-older-people.aspx

Exercises for suppleness

- http://www.nhs.uk/Livewell/fitness/Pages/flexibility-exercises-for-older-people.aspx

Feet (Physical well-being)

Your feet take around 8,000 steps a day. Are you paying enough attention to their care?

Find your care here...

- http://www.ageuk.org.uk/health-wellbeing/keeping-fit/fitter-feet

Good night's sleep (Physical well-being)

Are you getting a good night's sleep?

Find your care here...

- http://www.ageuk.org.uk/health-wellbeing/conditions-illnesses/getting-a-good-nights-sleep

Hair (Physical well-being)

Does your hair colour and style add years to your age or would a change make a difference?

Find your care here...

- http://www.nlm.nih.gov/medlineplus/ency/article/004005.htm

Image (Physical well-being)

Does the 'you' in your imagination reflect the 'you' in the mirror?

Find your care here...

- http://www.ageuk.org.uk/health-wellbeing/keeping-your-body-healthy/how-to-be-body-confident-in-later-life

Jokes (Social well-being)

Can you find your sense of humour every day?

Find your care here...

- http://www.enchantedlearning.com/jokes

Keeping connected (Social well-being)

Are you in contact with your local community and those around you?

Find your care here...

- http://www.ageuk.org.uk/health-wellbeing/relationships-and-family

Laughter (Social well-being)

Do you find something to laugh about every day?

Find your care here...

- http://www.laughteryoga.org/english

Memory (Mental well-being)

Do you walk into a room and forget why you have arrived there?

Find your care here...

- http://www.helpguide.org/articles/memory/how-to-improve-your-memory.htm

Nails (Physical well-being)

Are your nails softening and splitting?

Find your care here...

- http://www.nlm.nih.gov/medlineplus/ency/article/004005.htm

Outdoors (Spiritual well-being)

Do you take the time to go outside and appreciate the benefits of nature, seeing the sunrise, sunset and changing seasons?

Find your care here...

- http://www.ted.com/talks/the_lady_lifers

Posture (Physical well-being)

Do you notice your friends stooping as they walk? Are you doing this also?

Find your care here...

- http://www.nhs.uk/Livewell/Backpain/Pages/back-pain-and-common-posture-mistakes.aspx

Quiet time (Spiritual well-being)

Are you taking enough time for yourself to reflect on the day and write in your Happy Book? (Chapter 6)

Find your care here...

- http://www.actionforhappiness.org/10-keys-to-happier-living

Recreation (Spiritual well-being)

Are you having some fun and re-creation with the things you are doing every day?

Find your care here...

Wikipedia lists over 200 different hobbies as part of established organisations

- http://en.wikipedia.org/wiki/List_of_hobbies

Skin care (Physical well-being)

Your skin contains 16 pints or 9 litres of water. Are you replacing the moisture daily?

Find your care here...

- http://www.nia.nih.gov/health/publication/skin-care-and-aging

Teeth (Physical well-being)

You use your teeth just as much as you use your feet. Do you take enough care of them?

Find your care here...

- http://www.nia.nih.gov/health/publication/taking-care-your-teeth-and-mouth

Using all your senses (Physical well-being)

Are you consciously using your sense of touch, feel, smell, hearing and taste every day?

Find your care here...

- http://www.mindmapinspiration.com/how-to-heighten-your-senses-mind-map-paul-foreman/

Volunteering (Social well-being)

When you worked you went somewhere each day where you were expected. Do you miss that regular contact with folk?

Find your care here...

- http://www.do-it.org.uk/

Weight loss (Physical well-being)

Now that you have more time will losing weight become easier?

Find your care here...

- http://www.nhs.uk/Livewell/weight-loss-guide/Pages/losing-weight-getting-started.aspx

X factor (Spiritual well-being)

Are you using all your natural talents?

Find your care here...

- https://www.ted.com/talks/jane_fonda_life_s_third_act
- http://www.pursuit-of-happiness.org/science-of-happiness/

Your blessings (Spiritual well-being)

Do you count your blessings rather than your woes every day?

Find your care here...

- http://www.allgreatquotes.com/count_your_blessings_ quotes.shtml

Zing (Spiritual well-being)

Can you find enjoyment and enthusiasm in all you do? Do you end each day with a touch of zing?

Find your care here...

- http://www.ted.com/talks/isabel_allende_tells_tales_of_ passion?language=en

Visit www.retirementsunlimited.co.uk for

updates on the Daily Dose of Care links

Finally

At the start of the book I set out some common concerns that have been disclosed to me since I started to discuss openly with others my own reluctance to give up work and my fear of retirement. If you are a reluctant retiree I hope that reading through this book has provided some insight into your own feelings and helped you to better understand the reasons for your reluctance. The Pauses for Thought were intended to prompt your own self-reflection and provoke discussions with others.

If you are already a rejoicing retiree, with your retirement all mapped out, and you have still read through the book then I hope you have picked up some tips along the way that you can use yourself or pass on to others.

If you are nervous about retirement then I hope that you are now more confident and optimistic about the unlimited opportunities and adventures that lie ahead of you.

If you are already retired then I hope that this book has provided you with some new ideas and motivated you to make some changes if that was your intention.

One aim of this book was for you to find guidance to some common concerns:

○ 'My work colleagues have stopped emailing and phoning me and I no longer feel valued.' Rather than using retirement as an extended vacation, undertake activities that replicate the benefits that work gave you, such as self-esteem and status (Chapter 1)

○ 'I am being pulled in all directions doing things I really don't want to be doing.' Is this the routine you envisioned for yourself? Take ownership of the direction of your retirement and proactively pursue choices that will deliver your expectations rather than waiting for it to happen. If you had your own plan then there will not be the danger that you fall into someone else's routine. (Chapter 2)

○ 'I feel I am just filling up my days and keeping busy to avoid getting bored.' Suddenly you are having to fill forty hours per week that has been filled for you for many years. If you are someone who has had many things going on in your life other than work you may settle into a new routine rather quickly and easily. If you only had work as your major focus then this transitional phase will probably need much more effort and work and this phase will be much more demanding of a total make over. (Chapter 3)

○ 'I feel uncomfortable in the role of retiree and I don't know how to introduce myself when I meet someone new.' This is your opportunity to explore your authentic self rather

than just opting for the self we have shown the world so far
(Chapter 4)

○ 'My partner, my family and I are falling over ourselves and
falling out all the time.' Retirement brings changes for
everyone around you. Avoid conflict in long-standing
relationships by communicating concerns and changes
(Chapter 5)

○ 'I am just not enjoying my retirement in the way that I
expected to.' Expand your spheres of activity rather than
reducing your sphere of activity and contacts (Chapter 6)

○ 'Now that I am no longer working I feel there is little
meaning and purpose to my life.' Refuse to acknowledge
that retirement is about endings and accept that finding new
meaning and purpose is at the heart of a successful
retirement (Chapter 7)

○ 'Retirement is costing more than I budgeted for.' Tap into
imaginative income streams rather than just relying on
pensions and savings or acknowledge that what you have is
'enough'. (Chapter 8)

○ 'We have moved location but it is not turning out as
successful as we expected.' Having reflected on the true
reasons why you moved you may be able to adapt your new
location so that it is the home you always intended (Chapter 9)

○ 'I have often felt quite low since I retired.' Retirement gives
us the time to concentrate on all the aspects of our well-
being in a way that we might not have been able to focus

before. This includes our physical, mental, social and spiritual well-being. (Chapter 10)

A further aim was that when you finished reading this book you would have given yourself the time and space to:

- ○ Review your own personal expectations for a successful retirement
- ○ Seek guidance from those who have successfully retired before you
- ○ Devise strategies to manage the expectations others have of you
- ○ Systematically focus on facing your retirement concerns and fears
- ○ Revive personal passions and dreams
- ○ Prioritise meaning and purpose
- ○ Find entitlement to fun and enjoyment in retirement

In the following pages some of the *Pauses for Thought* are repeated so that you can see whether my aims have been met, and you have taken the opportunity to re-kindle old passions; explore wider horizons; meet new challenges; and find out who you really are. Compare the answers you would give today, now that you have had time to reflect, with those that you gave as you were reading through the book.

Reflections on CHAPTER 1 – REPLACEMENT

....

ORIGINAL PAUSE FOR THOUGHT

What benefits from work are you likely/do you miss the most?
How could you replace them?

NEW REFLECTIONS: *What steps have you taken to replace them?*

....

ORIGINAL PAUSE FOR THOUGHT

You were asked to divide this circle up into ten segments and write in each one of the ten fears that are the subject of this book. You were asked to make a small line to indicate your current level of satisfaction with each area (the further away from the centre the more satisfied you are)

These were:

1. My ability to replace my work benefits
2. The expectations I have of my retirement
3. How I will spend my time
4. My ability to replace my career identity with a new identity
5. My relationships
6. My daily level of enjoyment and happiness
7. Meaning and purpose in my life
8. My finances
9. Where I live now
10. My level of physical, mental and social well-being

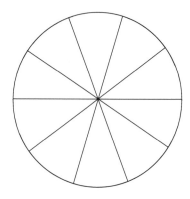

NEW REFLECTIONS: *Repeat this exercise now to see if your current level of satisfaction with each area has increased.*

....

ORIGINAL PAUSE FOR THOUGHT

What are the necessary components for a successful retirement for you?

NEW REFLECTIONS:

Have you changed your mind about the necessary components of a successful retirement for you?

What are the life positives you now see in your own retirement?

What are the life challenges you now see in your own retirement?

Reflections on CHAPTER 2 – EXPECTATIONS

....

ORIGINAL PAUSE FOR THOUGHT

What advice would you give to others in the future who maybe going through the transition from work to retirement?

NEW REFLECTIONS: Having been through the experience of retirement transition what advice would you give to others now?

Reflections on CHAPTER 3 – TIME

....

ORIGINAL PAUSE FOR THOUGHT

Is there anything you are still waiting for?
Will retiring bring it nearer?

NEW REFLECTIONS: Is it any nearer now?

....

ORIGINAL PAUSE FOR THOUGHT

What changes to your use of time would you like to make in retirement?

NEW REFLECTIONS:

What have you stopped doing?

What were the consequences?

How have you overcome the obstacles?

What have you done more of?

What were the consequences?

How have you overcome the obstacles?

What was not on your list that you have done?

Reflections on CHAPTER 4 – Identity

ORIGINAL PAUSE FOR THOUGHT

Who am I? Write down 10 facts about yourself

NEW REFLECTIONS: *Can you add to those facts?*

NEW REFLECTIONS:

My strengths are...

The talents I naturally give to others are...

The talents I most enjoy giving to others are...

NEW REFLECTIONS: *How do you introduce yourself to a stranger now?*

Reflections on CHAPTER 5 – RELATIONSHIPS

NEW REFLECTIONS: *Did you find replacements for the relationships you enjoyed at work?*

....

ORIGINAL PAUSE FOR THOUGHT

Choose four people who are important in your life

Which relationships feel most supportive?

What contribution do you make to those relationships?

Are there any relationships that are in need of work?

If so, what?

NEW REFLECTIONS: Has the situation changed at all?

NEW REFLECTIONS:

What was the result of your Expectations Exchange with:

> **Your partner**
> **Your children**
> **Your grandchildren (or their parents if appropriate)**
> **Your own parents and those of your partner**

....

ORIGINAL PAUSE FOR THOUGHT

I would like retirement to be a time in my life when...

I would like retirement to be a time in my life when I leave behind...

I would like retirement to be a time in my life when I take forward with me...

NEW REFLECTIONS:

Now I would like retirement to be a time in my life when...
Now I would like retirement to be a time in my life when I leave behind...
Now I would like retirement to be a time in my life when I take forward with me...

Reflections on CHAPTER 6 – ENJOYMENT AND HAPPINESS

ORIGINAL PAUSE FOR THOUGHT

Are you happier in some areas of your life than others?
Which are those areas? Why do you think that might be?
What do you think it will take to increase your enjoyment and your enduring level of happiness in those areas?

NEW REFLECTIONS:

What steps have you taken to increase your enjoyment and your enduring level of happiness in those areas?
Has it worked?
Have you increased the number of smiles you break into each day?

Have you increased the amount of laughter in your life each day?

Reflections on CHAPTER 7 – MEANING AND PURPOSE

NEW REFLECTIONS:
Are you doing what you really want to do with your retirement?
What steps have you taken to change the situation?

Reflections on CHAPTER 8 – ENOUGH

....

ORIGINAL PAUSE FOR THOUGHT
What does 'enough' mean to me?

NEW REFLECTIONS:
Would you answer that question in the same way now?
How accurate was your income and expenditure forecast?
Have you had to make any adjustments to your financial situation or any adjustments to your expectations?

Reflections on CHAPTER 9 – NEW LOCATION

NEW REFLECTIONS: How would you answer these questions now?

Home to me is...

What are the favourite spaces in your home?

What do you value most about your home and neighbourhood?

If you knew you were going to stay there for the rest of your life what changes would you make?

Reflections on CHAPTER 10 – TAKING CARE

NEW REFLECTIONS: *What daily doses have you been taking from your A-Z of Care?*

	Given high priority	Given some priority	Given low priority	Given no priority
Attitude				
Brain fitness				
Conversation				
Diet				
Exercise				
Feet				
Good night's sleep				
Hair				
Image				
Jokes				

	Given high priority	Given some priority	Given low priority	Given no priority
Keeping connected				
Laughter				
Memory				
Nails				
Outdoors				
Posture				
Quiet time				
Re-creation				
Skin care				
Teeth				
Using all your senses				
Volunteering				
Weight loss				
X factor				
Your blessings				
Did you find your zing?				

Remember the Spanish word
for retirement is jubilacion
so celebrate and enjoy it!

References

CHAPTER 1 – REPLACEMENT
How can I replace the benefits I get from work?

Age UK. *Later Life in the United Kingdom*. May 2015

European Commission. *The 2012 Ageing Report*

Johnson, Richard P. *The New Retirement*: Discovering Your Dream. St. Louis, Missouri: World Press, 2001

Johnson, Richard P. *What Color Is Your Retirement?* St. Louis, Missouri, World Press, 2006

Schlossberg, Nancy K. *Revitalising Retirement: Reshaping Your Identity, Relationships, and Purpose*. Washington: APA Life Tools, 2010

Zopa and Consumer Intelligence. *Pre-tirement not retirement*. December 2014

CHAPTER 2 – EXPECTATIONS
What can I expect from my transition from work to retirement?

Age UK. *Later Life in the United Kingdom. May 2015*

Bridges, William. *Transitions: Making Sense of Life's Changes*. Cambridge: Da Capo Press, 2004

Ebaugh, Helen Rose Fuchs. *Becoming an Ex: The Process of Role Exit*. Chicago: The University of Chicago Press, 1988

Johnson, Richard P. *The New Retirement: Discovering Your dream*. St Louis, Missouri World Press, 2001

Miller, Thomas W. *Handbook of Stressful Transitions Across the Lifespan*. New York: Springer, 2012

CHAPTER 3 – TIME
How will I spend my time?

Age UK. *Later Life in the United Kingdom. May 2015*

Kabat-Zinn, Jon. *Wherever You Go, There You are – Mindfulness Meditation for Everyday Life.* London: Piatkus Books Ltd, 1994

Saint Augustine. *Confessions.* London: Penguin Classics, 1961

Schlossberg, Nancy K. *Retire Smart Retire Happy: Finding Your True Path in Life.* APA Life Tools, 2009

Schlossberg, Nancy K. *Revitalising Retirement: Reshaping Your Identity, Relationships, and Purpose.* Washington: APA Life Tools, 2010

Smith, Mary Helen and Smith, Shuford. 101 Secrets for a Great Retirement: Practical Inspirational & Fun Ideas for the Best Years of Your Life. New York: McGraw-Hill, 2000

Taylor, Roberta K. and Mintzer, Dorian. *The Couple's Retirement Puzzle: 10 Must-Have Conversations for Transitioning to the Second Half of Life.* Waltham: Lincoln St. Press, 2011

Tolkein, JRR. *The Hobbit.* London: Harper Collins, 2013

Tolle, Eckhart. *The Power of Now: A Guide To Spiritual Enlightenment.* London: Hodder & Stoughton, 2011

Williams, Mark and Penman, Danny. *Mindfulness: A Practical Guide to Finding Peace in a Frantic World.* London: Piatkus, 2011

Zimbardo, Philip. *The Time Paradox. Using the new Psychology of Time to your Advantage.* Rider Ebury Publishing, 2008

CHAPTER 4 – IDENTITY
Who will I become once I am retired?

Age UK. *Later Life in the United Kingdom. May 2015*

Ellis, Albert. *Overcoming Resistance: Rational-Emotive Therapy with*

Difficult Clients. New York: Springer Publishing, 1985

Life Planning Network. *Live Smart After 50: The Experts' Guide to Life Planning for Uncertain Times.* Boston, 2013

Longhurst, Michael. *The Beginner's Guide to Retirement: Taking Control of Your Future.* Dublin: Newleaf, 2000

Schlossberg, Nancy K. *Revitalizing Retirement: Reshaping Your Identity, Relationships, and Purpose.* Washington: APA Life Tools, 2010

Stone, Marika and Howard. *Too Young to Retire: A Journal of Transition.* USA: 2Young2Retire Associates, 2006

Viorst, Judith. *Necessary Losses.* New York: Fireside, 1998

Zimbardo, Philip. *The Time Paradox: Using the new Psychology of Time to your advantage.* Rider Ebury Publishing, 2008

www.myers briggs.org

CHAPTER 5 – RELATIONSHIPS
How will my relationships change?

Age UK. *Later Life in the United Kingdom.* May 2015

Beach, Brian and Bamford, Sally-Marie. *Isolation: The emerging crisis for older men.* Independent Age.

Gutmann, David. *Reclaimed Powers: Men and Women in Later Life.* Illinois: Northwestern University Press, 1994

Johnson, Richard P. *What Color Is Your Retirement?.* St Louis, Missouri: Retirement Options, 2006

Life Planning Network. *Live Smart After 50: The Experts' Guide to Life Planning for Uncertain Times.* Boston: 2013

Schlossberg, Nancy K. *Retire Smart Retire Happy: Finding Your True Path in Life.* APA Life Tools, 2009

Schlossberg, Nancy K. *Revitalizing Retirement: Reshaping Your Identity, Relationships, and Purpose.* Washington: APA Life Tools, 2010

Smith, Mary Helen and Shuford. *101 Secrets for a Great Retirement: Practical, Inspirational & Fun Ideas for the Best Years of Your Life.* New York: McGraw-Hill, 2000

Sullivan, Daniel, Landau, Mark J., Rothschild, Zachary K. (2010). An Existential Function of Enemyship: Evidence That People Attribute Influence to Personal and Political Enemies to Compensate for Threats to Control. *Journal of Personality and Social Psychology,* Vol. 98, No. 3, 434-449

Taylor, Roberta K. and Mintzer, Dorian. *The Couple's Retirement Puzzle: 10 Must-Have Conversations for Transitioning to the Second Half of Life.* Waltham: Lincoln St. Press, 2011

Weiss, Robert S. (1974). The provisions of social relationships. In Z. Rubin (Ed.), *Doing unto others* (pp. 17-26). Englewood Cliffs, NJ: Prentice Hall.

Weiss, Robert S. and Bass, Scott A. *Challenges of the Third Age: Meaning and Purpose in Later Life.* New York: Oxford University Press, 2002

CHAPTER 6 – ENJOYMENT AND HAPPINESS
How can I find enjoyment and happiness in my retirement?

Csikszentmihalyi, Mihaly. *Flow – The classic work on how to achieve happiness.* USA: The Random House Group, 2002

Csikszentmihalyi, Mihaly. *Good Business: Leadership, Flow and the Making of Meaning.* USA: Hodder Paperbacks, 2004

James, William. *The Principles of Psychology Volume One.* New York: Dover Publications Inc., 2013

Kataria, Dr Madan. *The Inner Spirit of Laughter: Five Secrets from the Laughing Guru.* Bangalore: Dr Kakaria School of Laughter Yoga Publishing, 2012

Lyubomirsky, Sonja. *The How of Happiness: A Practical Guide to Getting the Life You Want.* London: Piatkus, 2013

Lyubomirsky, Sonja and Sheldon, Kennon M. and Schkade, David (2005) Pursuing Happiness: The Architecture of Sustainable Change. *Review of General Psychology Vol 9 No 2 111-131*

Lyle, Lesley. *Laugh Your Way To Happiness: Use the Science of Laughter for Total Well-being.* Oxford: Watkins Publishing, 2014

McKay, Helen F. *Links To Your Happiness.* New South Wales: Hightor Publishing, 2007

Maslow, A.H. (1943). A Theory of Human Motivation. *Psychological Review,* 50 pp. 370-396)

Schlossberg, Nancy K. *Retire Smart Retire Happy: Finding Your True Path in Life.* APA Life Tools, 2009

Seligman, Martin E.P. *Authentic Happiness.* London: Nicholas Brealey Publishing, 2005

Steakley, Lia. *Dream It. List It. How to Live a Bigger and Bolder Life from the Life List Experts at 43Things.com.* New York: Workman Publishing, 2008

Wolfe, W. Beran. *How to be Happy Though Human.* London: George Routledge & Sons Ltd. 1933

Zimbardo, Philip. *The Time Paradox: Using the new Psychology of Time to your advantage.* Rider Ebury Publishing, 2008 www.authentichappiness.org

CHAPTER 7 – MEANING AND PURPOSE
Will I find meaning and purpose in my retirement?

Frankl, Viktor E. *Man's Search for Meaning.* Rider Ebury Publishing, 2004

Harrold, Fiona. *Be Your Own Life Coach.* London: Hodder and Stoughton, 2001

Johnson, Richard P. What Color is Your Retirement? St Louise, Missouri: Retirement Options, 2006

Koltko-Rivera, Mark E. (2006). Rediscovering the Later Version of Maslow's Hierachy of Needs: Self-Transendence and Opportunities for Theory, Research, and Unification. – *Review of General Psychology,* Vol 10, No. 4,302-317

Life Planning Network. *Live Smart After 50: The Experts' Guide to Life Planning for Uncertain Times.* Boston: 2013

Maslow, A.H. (1943). A Theory of Human Motivation. *Psychological Review,* 50 pp. 370-396)

Schlossberg, Nancy K. *Revitalizing Retirement: Reshaping Your Identity, Relationships, and Purpose.* Washington: APA Life Tools, 2010

Seligman, Martin E.P. *Authentic Happiness.* London: Nicholas Brealey Publishing, 2005

Steakley, Lia. *Dream It. List It. How to Live a Bigger and Bolder Life from the Life List Experts at 43Things.com.* New York: Workman Publishing, 2008

The Independent Commission on Voluntary Sector and Ageing. *A Better Offer – The Future of Volunteering in an ageing society. August 2014* Ageing Society

Zelinski, Ernie J. *The Joy of Not Working: A book for the retired, unemployed, and overworked.* Berkeley: Ten Speed Press, 2003

CHAPTER 8 – ENOUGH
Will I have enough money to do what I want to do?

Age UK. *Later Life in the United Kingdom. May 2015*

Bach, David. *The Automatic Millionaire.* New York : Broadway Books, 2006

Hemingway, Ernest. *For Whom the Bell Tolls.* London: Arrow Books, 1994

Hoffman, Ellen. *The Retirement Catch-up Guide.* New York: Newmarket Press, 2000

Johnson, Richard P. *What Color Is Your Retirement?* St Louis, Missouri: Retirement Options, 2006

Johnson, Richard P. *The New Retirement: Discovering Your Dream.* St Louis, Missouri: World Press, 2001

Longhurst, Michael. *The Beginner's Guide to Retirement: Taking Control of Your Future.* Dublin: Newleaf, 2000

Lowe, Jonquil. *Be Your Own Financial Adviser.* Harlow: Pearson Education Ltd, 2010

Maslow, A.H. (1943). A Theory of Human Motivation. *Psychological Review*, 50 pp. 370-396)

Office for National Statistics. Family Spending 2013 http://www.ons.gov.uk/ons/search/index.html?newquery=retired+family+spending

Peeling, Nic. *Brilliant Retirement: Your practical guide to a happy, healthy, financially sound retirement.* Harlow. Pearson Education, 2010

Phillips, Michael. *The Seven Laws of Money.* Boston: Shambhala Publications Inc, 1993

Schlossberg, Nancy K. *Retire Smart Retire Happy: Finding Your True Path in Life.* APA Life Tools, 2009

Smith, Mary Helen and Shuford. *101 Secrets for a Great Retirement: Practical, Inspirational & Fun Ideas for the Best Years of Your Life.* New York: McGraw-Hill, 2000

Stone, Marika and Howard. *Too Young to Retire: 101 Ways to Start the Rest of Your Life.* New York: Plume, 2004

Zimbardo, Philip. *The Time Paradox: Using the new Psychology of Time to your advantage.* Rider Ebury Publishing, 2008

CHAPTER 9 – NEW LOCATION
Should I move somewhere new?

Age UK. *Later Life in the United Kingdom.* May 2015

Chartered Institute of Housing, *New Approaches to Housing for Older People,* June 2014

Doland, Erin Rooney. *Unclutter Your Life in One Week.* New York: Gallery Books, 2011

Life Planning Network. *Live Smart After 50: The Experts' Guide to Life Planning for Uncertain Times.* Boston, 2013

Longhurst, Michael. The Beginner's Guide to Retirement: Taking Control of Your Future. Dublin: Newleaf, 2000

Nolan, Clare. *Making a House Your Home.* London: Kyle Books, 2011

Older Women's Co-Housing development in High Barnet http://www.owch.org.uk.

Smith, Mary Helen and Shuford. *101 Secrets for a Great Retirement: Practical, Inspirational & Fun Ideas for the Best Years of Your Life.* New York: McGraw-Hill, 2000

Turner, Stuart. *Retirement Manual: Mid-life onwards.* Yeovil: Haynes Publishing, 2012

Vandervelde, Dr Maryanne. *Retirement for Two: Everything You Need To Know To Enjoy The Rest Of Your Lives Together.* London: Piatkus, 2005

Zelinski, Ernie J. *How To Retire Happy, Wild and Free.* Edmonton: VIP, 2010

Zimbardo, Philip. *The Time Paradox: Using the new Psychology of Time to your advantage.* Rider Ebury Publishing, 2008

CHAPTER 10 – TAKING CARE
How should I take care of myself?

Beare, Sally. *The Anti-ageing Diet*. London: Piatkus Books Ltd, 2006

Gibson Dr. H B. *A Little of What You Fancy Does You Good*. London: Third Age Press, 1997

Johnson, Richard P. *The New Retirement: Discovering Your Dream*. St Louis, Missouri: World Press, 2001

Johnson, Richard P. *What Color Is Your Retirement?*. St Louis, Missouri: Retirement Options, 2006

Katz, Lawrence C. and Rubin, Manning. *Keep Your Brain Alive*. New York: Workman Publishing, 2014

Knope Dr. Karl. *Stretching for 50+*. Berkeley: Ulysses Press, 2004

Knope Dr. Karl, *Weights for 50+*. Berkeley: Ulysses Press, 2006

Life Planning Network. *Live Smart After 50: The Experts' Guide to Life Planning for Uncertain Times*. Boston, 2013

Longhurst, Michael. *The Beginner's Guide to Retirement: Taking Control of Your Future*. Dublin: Newleaf, 2000

Lulu. *Lulu's Secret of Looking Good*. London: Collins, 2010

Moran, Diana. *Fresh Face – the easy way to look 10 years younger*. London: Hamlyn, 2005

Moran, Diana. *Live Longer Feel Younger Look Great*. Hamlyn, 2005

Smith, Mary Helen and Shuford. *101 Secrets for a Great Retirement: Practical, Inspirational & Fun Ideas for the Best Years of Your Life*. New York: McGraw-Hill, 2000

Stone, Marika and Howard. *Too Young to Retire: 101 Ways to Start the Rest of Your Life*. New York: Plume, 2004

Stone, Marika and Howard. *Too Young to Retire: A Journal of Transition*. USA: 2Young2Retire Associates, 2006

Twiggy. *A Guide to Looking And Feeling Fabulous Over Forty*. London: Penguin, 2008

Yabsley, Charmaine. *Natural Beauty Treatments*. Duncan Baird Publishers, 2005

Acknowledgements

I would like to thank

Dr Richard P Johnson and the team at Retirement Options (www.retirementoptions.com) and Dr Paul Ward of 2Young2Retire (www.2Young2Retire.com) for the mentorship and support given during their retirement coaching accreditation programmes;

The authors of the books and articles I consulted during my writing who gave me the inspiration for this book;

Eddie Calland, Janet Lange, Ian McMillan, Angela Murphy OBE, Keith Ridland, Sue Thompson and Mary Whittaker and others for their time in reading early drafts and providing invaluable feedback;

Lucy McCarraher and Darshana Ubl whose KPI (Key Person of Influence) programme prompted the creation of this book; also Tori Tulloch who recommended the programme; and Jenni Murray;

Helena, Harry, Nadia, Brian and Dorothy for their endless encouragement;

and my late Husband and my late Father, who are never far from my thoughts.

The Author

Pamela Houghton is a Retirement Coach and founder of Retirements Unlimited. She believes that retirement provides us with unlimited possibilities but taking full advantage of these opportunities requires planning. We are encouraged to plan our finances, but very often little thought is given to what we might actually do with our retirement. She works with clients who are soon to retire, or newly retired, embarking on the third stage of their life, to take the fear out of retirement. Together they explore existing retirement plans, find ways of replacing their career identity and discover exciting new possibilities.

For most of her career Pamela has worked within higher education. She started out as a Lecturer in European Business and progressed to creating and managing the Learning Development Unit for one of the largest Universities in the UK. She found the transition from leaving an intellectually challenging, exciting and fulfilling career to retirement was difficult.

As a result of her own experience of finding little support to help work through the issues thrown up by an earlier than expected retirement she decided to train as a Retirement Coach and gained accreditation with the leading US training organisations in this field.

Pamela Houghton can be contacted by email at pamhoughton@retirementsunlimited.co.uk or through her website www.retirementsunlimited.co.uk and would like to hear from you about your experiences of retirement.

Printed in Great Britain
by Amazon.co.uk, Ltd.,
Marston Gate.